When Someone You Love Is Dying

When Someone You Love Is Dying

David Clark, Ph.D.
Peter Emmett, M.D.

BETHANY HOUSE PUBLISHERS
MINNEAPOLIS, MINNESOTA 55438

Published by Bethany House Publishers
A Ministry of Bethany Fellowship International
11400 Hampshire Avenue South
Minneapolis, Minnesota 55438
www.bethanyhouse.com

Printed in the United States of America
ISBN 0–7642–2084–5

To
Bob Rakestraw,
colleague and friend

DAVID CLARK is a professor of theology at Bethel Theological Seminary in St. Paul, Minnesota. He is a popular speaker and author of five books. As the son of American missionaries in Tokyo, Japan, Dr. David Clark gained valuable cross-cultural experience during his growing-up years. He spent fifteen years in Asia before returning to the United States to continue his education at Trinity Evangelical Divinity School (M.A.) and Northwestern University (Ph.D.). He and his wife, Sandy, and their two sons live in St. Paul.

PETER EMMETT is currently pastor of West Harpswell Baptist Church in Maine. With twenty years of experience working at Eastern Maine Medical Center, twelve of those as Chief of Emergency Services, Dr. Peter Emmett saw firsthand the grief process a family goes through when a loved one is dying.

Contents

Introduction

Steve stared blankly out the window of the hospital room. As next of kin, Steve had taken responsibility for the personal affairs of his elderly uncle, Russ Thomason. Steve's lips trembled as he contemplated the doctor's words. This morning she had confirmed that Russ's life was ending. "Your uncle's body is no longer able to eliminate fluids," she said. "Unless we put Russ on an artificial kidney, he will die in a few weeks."

Always a vigorous man, Uncle Russ had lived alone since his wife died almost twelve years before. He quit teaching sixth graders a decade ago and now tended his garden and carved the occasional ax handle for a friend. Independent almost to a fault, he managed his meals and kept a spotless house. Just last December, he shoveled eight inches of snow to attend church one wintry Sunday. His faith in God saw him through a difficult life, and he believed his Lord would walk with him to the end.

About a year ago, Russ noticed blood in his urine. At Steve's prodding, he agreed to see his doctor, who discovered that the blood came from a malignant tumor in his left kidney. Tests showed no evidence that the malignancy had spread to other parts of the body. The surgeon removed the diseased kidney and Russ started receiving chemotherapy. Russ tolerated the treatments well enough, but he never seemed to recover fully.

Russ had recently lost a lot of weight and was experiencing frequent, severe headaches. His memory was also failing. A few days before Russ came to the hospital, Steve stopped for a visit. He found supper turning black on the stove and Russ asleep in his chair. Reluctantly, Russ agreed to further tests. They revealed what everyone privately feared. The cancer had spread to Russ's brain and to his remaining, now failing, kidney. His doctor put him on medication to reduce the tumor and alleviate the headaches. She urged Russ not to live alone, but the old man refused her advice. Soon, however, his condition worsened, and Steve helped Russ with his admission to the hospital.

Russ coughed weakly, interrupting Steve's thoughts. He looked at his uncle. Russ had lost forty pounds. Steve struggled to convince himself that the man in that bed really was his Uncle Russ—the spirited gentleman who taught him to tie flies and track white-tailed deer, the one who took him to church and wrestled through Steve's tough questions about faith. Occasionally Russ groaned, seeming to mutter some words, but they made no sense.

Steve turned the doctor's statements over and over in

his mind. *Your uncle's body can no longer eliminate fluids,* the doctor had said. *Unless we put Russ on an artificial kidney, he will die in a few weeks.* But what kind of life would dialysis give him? Would it simply prolong the dying? Because the cancer had spread to his brain, Russ might never regain coherence. Somehow, Steve thought, using the artificial kidney to lengthen Uncle Russ's life was like keeping a corpse alive.

Steve's sisters, Mary and Jan, were Russ's only other living relatives. As a private man, their uncle had never revealed what he wanted done should this situation arise. The vigor of his life, in fact, had suggested he would never be this incapacitated, this vulnerable. But what had seemed impossible was now real, and Steve and his sisters faced a decision about their uncle's fate.

Steve turned again toward the window. He wondered what Uncle Russ would say if he could advise them what to do. Would he say, as Steve was inclined to think, "I've prepared for this moment, kids. My faith was made for times like this. Please, no useless treatments. When it's my time to go, just let me go"? Russ had lived a long and robust life, and Steve felt dialysis would only prolong his dying. Ceasing useless medical treatments and focusing on what Uncle Russ now needed most—their love and care until death came—was surely the best path. A decision to *let go of* Uncle Russ seemed right.

Mary was never close to her uncle, and because she lived in another state, she hadn't seen him for several years. Though she was genuinely pained to see her uncle in this condition, she matter-of-factly told the doctor what she thought they should do. If the doctor was certain there was medically nothing more to do to give good life to Uncle Russ, they should save the grief and expense of further attempts to prolong his life. She even asked whether the doctor could hasten Uncle Russ's death: "Could you do something to make this easier for all of us?" Mary wanted to relieve Russ of the suffering he might have to endure—beyond that, she wanted to take matters into her own hands and hasten death. Steve realized Mary wanted to *dispose of* her uncle as quickly and painlessly as possible.

Jan, their younger sister, had no question about what to do. She hated the thought of losing her favorite uncle. She wanted him started on dialysis immediately. She insisted the doctor try an experimental drug she had read about in *McCall's*. Though she had no evidence that it would help him—it would probably make him sicker—Jan insisted that the medical staff try everything possible. "Life is precious, and as long as God gives it," she reasoned, "we must do all we can to keep it. We should stop at nothing. Something just might work. In the meanwhile, maybe God will do a miracle." Steve believed Jan wanted to *hold on to* Uncle Russ even though there was no medical hope of recovery.

To himself, Steve noted the irony that Mary and Jan, with their opposite agendas, each wanted to control the situation.

Somehow Steve and his sisters would struggle to a decision. Their dilemma was laced with questions—ethical, legal, medical, psychological, biblical, theological. They had to consider what was right in the light of all these factors. Perhaps you will, too. In a world of high-tech medicine, the approaching death of a loved one from an accident or apparently terminal illness thrusts complex decisions on many families. Do we *hold on to* our loved ones, as Jan proposed—insisting on medical treatment to the bitter end? Do we *dispose of* our loved ones, as Mary advocated—ending the lives of loved ones to relieve suffering? Or do we *let go of* our loved ones as Steve advised—turning from useless medical treatments to emotional and spiritual caring until death comes of its own accord?

We defend the third approach. There's never a time to stop caring. But there does come a time to let go. Why do we say this? And how can we know when this time has come? Where do God's purposes for suffering enter in? How can we cease attempts to cure given what the Bible teaches about life and death? How can we make difficult, end-of-life decisions? If you have an "Uncle Russ" of your own, if you work in the medical profession, or if you're a person who simply cares about applying God's truth to everyday life—you're probably asking similar questions. Our reason for writing is to share with you some balanced, compassionate answers from the Bible to these tough questions.

In order to give you the information you'll need, we're going to discuss several topics. First, some key foundational issues. Some think that health care is health care—that there's only one way to think about it! But people actually hold widely varying attitudes toward medicine. In chapter 1, we'll show you what you can expect of health care—its goals and limitations.

Second, as you face tough, real-life questions, you will find some people claiming that ethical decisions can be made based on simplistic formulas. Others don't quite know where to begin and never arrive at any helpful conclusion. Moral issues are indeed complex, and end-of-life decisions among the most difficult. In chapter 2, we share some straightforward things you need to consider in making ethical choices, and we give you a series of steps you can work through to make a morally right choice.

Third, good decisions defend deep values. For example, "Do not commit adultery" isn't a negative rule that prohibits the good life, but a positive principle that protects the value of married love. In chapter 3, we help you understand why, from God's point of view, the sanctity of human life is such a fundamental value.

Fourth, we discuss the meaning of death. After all, if life is so good, how should we understand death? In chapter 4, we'll show you how to make sense out of the relationship between soul and body.

Fifth, everyone's heard news reports about mercy killing and physician-assisted suicide. While many people defend these ideas, chapter 5 offers strong reasons not to go that way.

Sixth, if we argue that euthanasia isn't a good idea, it might seem that we don't care about people's dying painful deaths. But we want you to know that there are good alternatives. The hospice movement we describe in chapter 6 helps us to say "good-bye" to our loved ones even as we ease their suffering. If you have loved ones unable to make decisions about their medical care, we'll provide helpful information about the legal options open to your family.

Seventh, even under the best circumstances, facing death raises questions about suffering. Both patients and families ask how God expects us to handle pain. In chapter 7, we offer you some comforting thoughts on this age-old question.

Eighth, even if you trust God, it's still important to prepare for death. In chapter 8, we'll discuss several key things to ponder in preparation for the end.

And finally, as we approach death, the biggest issue is preparing to meet God. Lots of people have their own ideas about this. But in chapter 9, we will present a practical understanding of what the Bible says about being at peace with God. The thought of dying excites no one. But those who are at peace with their families and with God can die well. Death is a moment that tests true faith, and whether you are a patient or a family member, we'll paint for you a picture of the faith that can prepare each of us to meet God.

one

Can We Make Good Medicine Better?

Just as Steve and his sisters struggled over how to help Uncle Russ, people everywhere are grappling with shifting attitudes about health and curing. A contributor to *Newsweek*'s "My Turn" column clearly illustrates this point. A vet "put away" her ailing cat, she writes, sparing the animal much pain. Then she applies the same logic to human beings. Surely we could alleviate much suffering, she reasons. Now you might think she is worried about someone on the brink of an agonizing death.

But instead, she describes Henry, a mentally impaired man prone to violent outbursts. Why not kill him? It's surely the humane thing to do. "Why can't we treat fellow humans as humanely as we treat our pets?" she argues.[1]

Where Is My Doctor Coming From?

Our culture is moving away from traditional values in medicine. There's a growing sympathy for euthanasia, or mercy-killing, for example, and it's no longer limited to helping the terminally ill who suffer unbearable pain. Some now speak openly about euthanasia as an option for people who believe their lives aren't worth living. On other fronts, alternative medicine and managed health care are rewriting the rules of what constitutes "good" medicine. But these new movements don't necessarily guard your interests as a recipient of health care. They won't automatically result in the best care for your loved one. As you embark on making wise end-of-life decisions, it is crucial to understand where your doctor is coming from.

The Values of Modern Medicine

More than at any time in history, doctors are forging new values and beliefs. Early scientists saw a tight connection between their science and their faith in God. But since at least the 1700s—the Enlightenment period— the Western world has become increasingly secular, distancing itself from belief in God and his compassionate involvement in our world. These secular values often influence how doctors approach the practice of medicine, and their effect often goes unnoticed. Unfortunately, what results is that people today often presume that science should blindly pursue secular goals like absolute freedom of choice and personal success. In other words, we want perfect control over health and life and death—and we want it now! Science and medicine have become chauffeurs of individualism, transporting people to their self-chosen destinations. Westerners now live "by the assumption that we must control our existence by acquiring the power to eradicate from our lives anything that threatens our autonomy as individuals."[2]

Few acknowledge the unexamined attitudes about life and death, about health, illness, and suffering that permeate health care. Let's give an example. We tend to split the body away from the spirit. And then we assume that medical science deals only with the physical—which explains how doctors trained in the best of schools can lack a bedside manner that attends to the human heart and soul.[3] Counting only the physical part of life as important means we define the word *life* solely in biological terms. *Death* becomes just the ending of *physical* life. *Healthy* comes to mean *physically* healthy. So a moral midget competing in a "World's Strongest Man" contest is counted as *healthy*. But a spiritual giant with Parkinson's isn't. Illness becomes the enemy of life, and suffering is a worthless and meaningless by-product of illness. After all, how could suffering be beneficial if physical well-being and the various pleasures and experiences it makes possible are what we treasure most?

Our language reveals our deepest attitudes. Mild illness is a "nuisance," and intense suffering is "pointless" because each saps physical vigor. My doctor's "job" is to fix these problems—to make them go away. (If I asked someone at City Hall to "fix" my speeding ticket, I'd be asking him to make it disappear.)[4] So if medicine can't cure a patient's body, then that person is in a "hopeless" situation, and the doctor reluctantly confesses failure: "There's nothing more I can reasonably do."

When doctors can no longer cure and death is inevitable, some patients and families attempt to maintain personal control by asserting an absolute right to decide how life will end. This is the logic of euthanasia and physician-assisted suicide (PAS). If we can't defeat disease and death, at least we can spit in the face of fate. We can wrestle meaning from meaningless suffering by a bold act of will. The desire to legalize euthanasia and PAS "rests upon precisely the same assumptions about human need, health, and the role of medicine that have created our present crisis—the right to, and necessity of, full control over our fate."[5] In our secular times, the values of unblemished health, individual freedom, and personal control stand at the top of our list.

The Wide Influence of Secular Values

Some people will say we have overstated our case. They might argue for this approach: Medicine uses neutral tools to reach good goals. And there's nothing wrong with using tools. A baseball bat, when used by a YMCA staffer to teach kids about teamwork, determination, and fair play, is good. The same bat, used by a criminal to attack and rob an elderly man, isn't. Similarly, we can judge the moral worth of medicine only by looking at the purpose for which its tools are used. The good or bad of medicine comes out only as we consider its results. Thus, some reason that medicine is neutral, and so Christians can use it to seek Christian ends.

We admit we have stated our view boldly. But to think that medicine is completely neutral is naïve. Many Christians, doctors included, hold some of the cultural values we just described in an inconsistent mix right alongside more obviously Christian attitudes. Some secular doctors adopt certain religious values simply because they're part of cultural tradition. Among both believers and nonbelievers, a secular philosophy in its purest form is rare. Yet Christians can adopt secular values without thinking. When facing a crisis, we too often find ourselves assuming that physical health, individual freedom, and complete control over our circumstances should be our most important concerns. What we might miss is finding the *right* thing to do and the *good* way to conduct ourselves. We may also miss God's provision to endure illness triumphantly and, if necessary, to die with grace.

What Alternative Medicine Teaches

Christians aren't the only critics of secular medicine, with its emphasis on the physical. Advocates of what is popularly known as "alternative medicine" strongly denounce the medical status quo. Alternative medicine draws insights from many sources, especially traditional and Asian cultures. Basic to alternative medicine is the concept of *organism*. An organism is a complicated reality where all of many parts affect all the other parts. According to alternative medicine, human beings in their environments are organisms, and all medical care must acknowledge this reality. A person isn't just a body—a self-contained physical machine. Each person has a psychological and a spiritual dimension. A human being is like a frog in a pond, in a valley, on a continent, on a planet, in a universe. If I was to care for that frog, I'd need to take that whole network into account.

The key to this view is seeing connections between the body and the soul. This means that alternative medicine pays attention not only to physical but also to spiritual, emotional, and attitudinal aspects of health. The phrase *holistic health* captures this idea. The body can't be well until both soul and mind are well—and until the three are in a delicate, balanced relationship. Wellness is a positive state of health, not merely the absence of disease, and it involves the whole organism, not the body alone. So alternative medicine stresses the patient's responsibility for health, as well as preventive care over and against remedial care, natural forms of healing and health, and spirituality as an aspect of health care.[6]

As a reaction against secular views of medicine, alternative medicine has some appeal to Christians. In some important ways, this reaction is right. As God created humans, the spiritual and the physical do interact. In this area, a Christian view of things is more consistent with holistic medicine than with secular medicine.

Alternative medicine, however, like secularized modern medicine, often strives to achieve individualism and personal control. Oddly, those who practice alternative medicine often employ the holistic philosophy of the East to achieve the values of the self-absorbed, secular West. In this way, alternative medicine reveals its true colors. Although alternative medicine promotes meditation over medication, its goals remain remarkably Western.

Alternative medicine, like secular medicine, displaces God from his rightful place in the medical process. Alternative medicine usually assumes that God and humans are aspects of the same whole or system. *God* is in an organic union with human persons. In this view, God isn't the supernatural creator the Bible says he is! Although we admire some of the pieces of alternative medicine—its stress on healthful living and preventive care, for instance—we need a more fully biblical perspective.

Managed Health Care

Secularized and alternative approaches to medicine are both influenced by the business-oriented values that have infiltrated our health care system.

Ten years ago a friend of mine had her first child in a large, West Coast hospital. At the forefront of managed care, the hospital, says my friend, "had all the nurturing qualities of an auto quick-lube shop." She was shuffled from building to building for routine tests and saw a different doctor for each prenatal visit. The system was barely adequate when what she needed was preventive maintenance—and altogether inadequate when she was confronted with an emergency cesarean section in which the anesthesia didn't take. Today this hospital has embarked on a ten-year program to change the callous attitudes of its workers toward patients.

The secular mentality tends to see the physician-patient relationship as a contract. In business contracts, two parties agree to exchange a product or service for a fee. In such an arrangement, long-term, personal loyalty isn't necessary, and each person acts to benefit himself. This doesn't mean that everyone breaks contracts willy-nilly, of course. In the long run, breaking contracts leads to financial ruin, while honoring contracts promotes the business self-interests of all. People keep contracts not primarily because they are loyal to other persons but to maintain the business climate in which they themselves can benefit.

Contract-oriented values have infiltrated our health care system. Notice that we use consumer-oriented language when describing health care *consumers* and health care *providers*. A health care *provider* is product-oriented. He offers a service and charges a fee. He may not be interested first and foremost in caring for people. I know of a dental clinic, for example, that pushes its employees to treat as many patients as possible and to recommend expensive treatments that are only marginally necessary. If you were a patient at this clinic, you would experience a doctor-patient relationship corrupted by economically oriented values.

Is There a Better View of Medicine?

Hidden influences shape our attitudes toward medicine. These cultural influences feel as natural to us as wetness feels to a fish. Since the fish doesn't know anything other than wetness, it never occurs to the fish that he shouldn't feel wet. Similarly, we don't realize that there are perspectives on health care other than what our culture considers normal.

Health care can be more than what contemporary medicine generally offers. As a distinctive approach to medicine, what we can call the "covenant care" view begins with a different perspective on life. A religious person can work out an understanding of medicine that reflects God's values. All Christians who receive medical treatment or who work in medicine or who provide care to a loved one can approach medical care with a distinctively Christian attitude. Of course, a believing doctor and an atheist colleague may prescribe the same antibiotic for two patients afflicted by the same bacterial infection. The difference, however, isn't always in what they do, but sometimes in the physician's or patient's attitudes and goals. (We will explain this more in chapter 2.) For the Christian, the practice of medicine, like every other aspect of life, expresses a godly view of life. We are God's children, created to love and to be loved by him.

This Christian understanding is vastly different from the contract mentality of today's medicine. At its center, good medicine is based on *covenant*. Covenants are serious, binding, long-term agreements. More than that, they intend good for each party and pledge an inner loyalty between the two parties. The Bible briefly mentions ceremonies that confirm covenants (Genesis 15:1–21). In ancient times, covenants were marked by ritual acts that indicated the serious nature of the agreement (Exodus 24:1–11). God made a number of specific covenants that affected both individuals and groups (Genesis 12:1–3; 15:1–21; 17:1–22). In the Old Testament, *covenant* describes the whole of God's good relationship to his people (Genesis 6:18; 9:8–17).

Covenant care is the "something more" we often find missing in medicine. When we face a loved one's likely death, we want more than technology. We want more than proficiency. We certainly want more than to enrich the health care system. We want our loved one *cured*. But whether or not that happens, we want our loved one *cared for*. Covenant provides the caring surroundings that can be curative when there is any chance of healing.[7] But it also offers relationships that are truly comforting when death nears.

God's covenant-making sums up the characteristic idea of love in the Old Testament: *hesed*, or covenant love. *Hesed* strongly emphasizes personal relationship with and faithfulness to others.[8] God created us to enjoy loving relationships. These require faithfulness and personal loyalty. The physician-patient relationship is just one example of this general idea. But covenant-quality care isn't just for doctors. It is the care with which we want to surround our suffering loved ones. No more than medical personnel, family members must not "fix" their relative or "do their time" caring and then get on with life.

Some reject covenant care medicine as unrealistic. After all, they declare, a hospital, clinic, or private practice is a business that must remain economically viable. This, of course, is true. But medical practice motivated by fee alone isn't good medicine—or fully Christian, even if the persons involved are Christians. Doctors and nurses should see their work with patients as an implicit covenant. Their primary motive is to serve and glorify God by responding knowledgeably, compassionately, and faithfully to patients.

Others may recognize that a contract philosophy dominates medical practice and yet see no way out. They claim that the institutional nature of medicine forces a contract-oriented view of things. But we believe that a God-centered, covenant-motivated practice is possible. Medicine isn't simply a matter of technique; it's an art of ministering to persons. Caregivers who cultivate the habit of seeing each patient as a person whom God loves—rather than as a body that needs repair—truly move toward an eminently good and biblical practice of medicine.

What Can I Expect From My Doctor?

If you are in the process of selecting health care for yourself or someone else, the idea of covenant care can help you find the best health care. Or it can help you develop the best relationship with the doctor you already work with.

Let's look at the practical issues of the type of care you need. A covenant care orientation in medicine promotes right action even as it keeps service to persons at the forefront. It includes two basic sets of principles. The first set of principles outlines the duties of professionals in health care, and the second set highlights the rights of their patients.

Doing No Harm and Doing Good

Following medical tradition, competent doctors and nurses follow two basic principles. The first says, "First, do no harm." (The technical term is *non-maleficence*.) *Non-maleficence* means we have a duty not to harm or kill others.[9] A doctor who heeds the principle of non-maleficence will choose *not* to treat a patient rather than pursue treatments that worsen a patient's condition with no realistic chance of improving health. A good doctor may, however, prescribe a painful course of chemotherapy that takes a patient "to hell and back" if it has sufficient likelihood of pushing cancer into remission.

The second says, "Seek only what's good" for the patient. (The technical term here is *beneficence*.) *Beneficence* expresses the biblical idea of *agape*, divine love, which means "willing what's good for the other." It flows from *hesed*, covenant love. Beneficence grounds love for the other in a faithful relationship. Like non-maleficence, beneficence is a basic principle of ethics. But the principle does raise questions. What happens if a patient wants to do what is clearly not in his own best interest? Does a doctor agree to do whatever the *patient thinks* is in his own interest, or should a doctor do what *she thinks*, as a medical professional, is in the patient's best interest? This question shows that beneficence functions in tension with some other principles that govern the rights of patients.

Autonomy and Paternalism

While medical personnel are trained to follow non-maleficence and beneficence—principles that protect the rights of patients—in the covenant care model, genuine *hesed* for others also requires respect for the autonomy and well-being of others.[10] In other words, physicians and nurses shouldn't seek their own goals—like career advancement or financial gain—by treating patients as *things*. Patients are *persons* who have their own goals for life. If someone uses another person as a means to achieving his own goals, he enters a contractual arrangement that belittles both parties.

Autonomy is the right of a person to demand respect, to govern herself under God. It's "being one's own person, without constraints either by another's action or by psychological or physical limitations."[11] In this sense, an autonomous person may choose her own life's path. She possesses moral permission to plan a course of action and to apply her own resources to carry out that plan. She's exercising *moral autonomy*: the moral right to govern her own life.

Of course, some people are unable to fulfill this right. *Factual autonomy*, the actual ability to fulfill *moral autonomy*, assumes both the skill and the opportunity to function as a fully adult human being. Obviously, people may have more or less factual self-rule. Some people have relatively less real freedom because they lack the ability to create and execute a plan of action. Children can't function independently because they lack the needed skills. If they grow up, they will learn to think ahead and carry out plans—in other words, they will become adults.

When a parent limits his child's freedoms, his limitation is morally justifiable and practically necessary. But restricting the liberty of a competent adult, as though the adult were a child, is *paternalism* in the negative sense of that word. An adult son of an aging widow, for example, might choose the apartment complex she will live in without consulting her. Paternalism toward adults is out of line. It neglects the right to independence that mature persons possess simply because they're adults. To treat a mature person paternalistically is to fail to respect—and therefore, to fail to love—that adult person.

To treat a child in a properly paternalistic way is loving. As we will see in later chapters, making choices for incapacitated adults is sometimes necessary. But families act wrongly when they foist decisions on an ill or injured loved one who is capable of making decisions. With most adults, "Doctor knows best" is not the best policy.

The Balancing Act: Informed Consent

The important principle of *informed consent* protects the basic principle of autonomy and limits unwarranted paternalism. In the past, most patients just assumed that physicians would provide benevolently for their medical needs. Today, however, people believe that patients should participate in treatment decisions.

The principle of informed consent became important as social critics and legal experts thought about everything from civil rights and consumer movements to the rights of prisoners and the incompetent and the atrocities of the Nazis.[12] *Informed consent* means that patients freely agree to treatment (*consent*) after they understand the medical staff's explanations of the risks and benefits (*informed*). Of course, a physician couldn't possibly explain all the information relating to a specific decision. Few patients know enough to understand everything about a medical procedure. In fact, most patients don't want to be burdened with all the details—including the often frightening list of possible complications. But patients do have to know something about the pros and cons of treatment before they agree to it.

In a healthy doctor/patient relationship, informed consent is more than the formality of reciting the pros and cons and signing a disclosure statement. The spirit of informed consent says it's okay to ask questions, to obtain second opinions, or to request consultations between doctors.

Informed consent acts like a referee between autonomy and paternalism. Too much paternalism and too little autonomy means the doctor appears to act beneficently, but may actually treat the patient with little respect. This is unfair to the patient. Too much autonomy and too little paternalism means the patient pressures the physician to provide treatments the patient doesn't understand or to write prescriptions that aren't in the patient's best interest. This is unfair to the doctor. Informed consent places responsibilities on both partners in the covenant care relationship. And so it protects, in a balanced way, the rights and knowledge of the medical staff on the one side, and the needs of the patients and their families on the other.

So how can you make such decisions in ways that affirm human life and honor God? That's what this book is all about.

Conclusion

Getting the best medical care is more than picking a good doctor or hospital. Covenant care is a way of viewing health and illness that shapes the rest of what we have to say—and all our suggestions for making wise decisions at the end of life. While the values that shape a covenant care view of medical practice and relationships come from the Bible, they meet the deepest needs of all people.

Once we accept a covenant perspective, we should then try to apply covenant values to decisions about medical treatment. So we will next address issues of how to make good ethical choices. While it's tempting to move quickly to discussions of practical examples and "for instances" that surround end-of-life decisions, we first want to discuss how to make moral decisions. What are the basic parts of good moral decisions that will benefit your loved one? What are the proper steps for making ethical decisions? Is ethics simply a matter of following rules, or is there more to it than that?

two

Are Moral Questions Answerable?

We know a professor of ethics who refuses to teach about specific ethical issues such as euthanasia. So complicated is the field of ethics, he says, that all he can do is discuss ethical theories. In class, he won't address concrete moral problems—real-life situations that need real-life solutions—because he insists that no one can make specific moral decisions until he knows an issue exhaustively. Ironically, this man teaches not at a university but at a seminary. He teaches not graduate students headed toward professional academics but Christian leaders called to ministry! Obviously and unfortunately, his approach leaves students unequipped to come alongside people faced with agonizing end-of-life questions.

We recognize a kernel of truth in what this professor says: Discerning right from wrong is sometimes difficult. But none of us has the luxury of ducking tough moral issues. We all face lifelong choices about love, work, and family. And sooner or later most of us face life-or-death decisions about ourselves or a loved one. Often these decisions need to be made in a matter of days, hours, even minutes—not over the span of a semester or the course of an academic career.

Moreover, in medical decision-making, there may be a clash of values between physician and patient or family, or within a family. A Christian might disagree with a non-Christian. So Christians faced with making these difficult end-of-life medical decisions must think about the basic values out of which treatment choices grow.

Thinkers who focus on ethics have proposed many different approaches to making moral decisions, and yet thorny problems remain.[1] Still, we believe we can develop a good process of ethical decision-making that works for real-life issues. In our view, thinking well often means taking a balanced position between two extremes. In defending a middle way in processing moral issues, we're vulnerable to criticism from all directions. So we will lay out this process, knowing that we face perils like those encountered by the man standing on the center line of a highway. The danger there, a proverb reminds us, is that he risks being hit by trucks going both ways.

How Do People Make Ethical Decisions?

We will highlight three tensions in making ethical choices. Although these tensions reflect different schools of thought in ethics, we suspect you will recognize the everyday opinions within your family or your own conflicting thoughts as we flesh out an ethical approach—an approach consistent with our Christian heritage and applicable to the end-of-life ethical questions we face. At the end of the chapter we offer a step-by-step guide to decision-making.

Situations and Principles

One basic question faced by all decision-makers is this: Is there a principle that fits this setting? There's another side to that question, however: What's unique about this situation?

A *principial* approach to ethics assumes that moral situations are enough alike that we can put all similar cases—all instances of murder, for example—in a single group. Once we collect identical moral acts into a class, we then apply a single rule to them all. We can live and make decisions based on principles. In contrast, *situationism* (also called *contextualism*) holds that every concrete moral decision is *so* unique, *so* particular, that we must decide each one on its own terms. According to situationism, because each moral problem is different, good ethical thinking can't simply apply exceptionless rules to concrete moral situations in a blanket way.

Think, for example, about the seventh commandment: "You shall not commit adultery" (Exodus 20:14). A principial approach takes all cases of adultery, places them into a group or class, and applies the seventh commandment to them all. As I consider the moral rightness of a certain action, I ask whether it fits in the class of adulterous acts. If it does, I simply apply the rule that's relevant to all actions of adultery, namely, the seventh commandment. This procedure yields a clear result: the action I'm pondering is morally wrong. In this way, we may use laws, norms, or rules to guide behaviors.

A wife who is having an affair, however, can list all sorts of personal reasons why *her* adultery is right: "My husband doesn't love me anymore." "He tells me I'm ugly." "He doesn't spend any time with the kids." Situationalism similarly resists norms, rules, or laws, and it assesses situations on a case-by-case basis.[2] In thinking through the seventh commandment, a situationalist insists that not all cases of adultery are alike. He or she would say that, of course, many acts of adultery are morally wrong (if they involve betraying a spouse in exchange for fleeting personal pleasure). But some cases may have extenuating circumstances that good ethical thinking should consider. So in situationism, the seventh commandment is only a helpful rule of thumb. It may rightly guide us in many situations, but it isn't an exceptionless or unbreakable law. It isn't an absolute command; it's more like a rule of strategy in a game.

An obvious parallel is "Thou shalt not kill," and its flip side, "Preserve life." Within a situationalist framework, there are any number of reasons to do otherwise. Someone actively looking to end a life can find countless justifications to do so. A situationalist sees principles as guidelines, such as "Punt on fourth down." In football, a team will usually kick the ball to the other team on fourth down rather than giving up the ball closer to its own goal line. At the end of a game, however, a team that's behind won't punt on fourth down. That almost guarantees a loss. In that situation, the coach ignores what's normally good advice ("Punt on fourth down") and knowingly does the risky thing. The risky strategy is preferable to certain defeat. Similarly, although most cases of adultery are morally wrong, according to situationism, occasionally a special situation requires a different assessment.[3]

This approach to moral thinking has severe problems. Common sense and moral reasoning offer us principles to live by. In the Bible, God sets wise, specific boundaries to our freedom. When we disregard moral authority, however, we appoint ourselves arbiters of right and wrong. We might say that what *feels* good *is* good. We might measure the rightness of a decision solely by results—but that creates other problems, as we will see. As humans we easily find reasons that we think justify breaking the rules of life, and so gone are any hard-and-fast limits to harmful behavior.

We reject situationism as a reliable guide to determining right and wrong. Principial ethics see God's commands as *absolutes*, exceptionless norms, a view held by most Christians. They're broad moral guidelines such as "Love your neighbor as yourself" (Matthew 22:39). Not every rule is an absolute, however. Some rules apply only to certain cultures (e.g., "Drive on the right side of the road" or, in Bible times, "Don't eat meat offered to idols"). But generally, principial approaches see ethical thinking as rightly classing acts into groups and then applying moral principles or rules to those classes. Seldom are the facts of two situations identical. Yet never are they completely unique or beyond the reasonable application of biblical principle.

So is it important to think about the unique facts of specific situations? Considering the facts of a situation is still essential to good ethical analysis. One can't make moral judgments about specific cases without looking at all relevant details. In making end-of-life decisions, this means that the likely result of a certain treatment decision—the medical prognosis—includes medical facts unique to the situation. We must consider these facts in making moral decisions. As Christians, we have the duty to love our neighbor. This is an absolute of Christian ethics. Now the question is, *How* shall we love him? The norm of love says we should always give life-saving medication. But we withhold medication in situations where it would do no good and would cause additional suffering. Or we might make different life-and-death decisions on behalf of a twelve-year-old than those made for an eighty-year-old; more aggressive, last-resort medical treatments, for example, might be risked for a younger person.

The facts of a situation *define the circumstances within which we must decide* what specific course of action biblical principles require us to take. Clear thinking emphasizes basic principles, but it must consider situational facts.

Results and Duties

A second basic question for ethical thinking is this: What role do results play in decision-making? Two questions emerge: What good will a particular act do? Is that the same as the right thing to do?

A result-oriented view of ethics determines rightness and wrongness by looking to the results of actions. It's a pragmatic view that examines the consequences or outcomes that an act produces in order to decide whether that action is good.[4] Here's an example: If I want to know whether I should give a destitute person some money to buy food, I think about results. I consider what the gift will do to myself, to those for whom I'm responsible, and to the person who's down on his luck. If the gift will only make that individual more dependent on me, it might be wrong to give it. If it will save his life, however, it might be wrong *not* to give it.

In contrast to result-oriented views are approaches that stress the obligation to do one's duty.[5] In systems of this kind, identifying right choices may depend to some degree on assessing results, but consequences can't by themselves tell what's right. To find the right decision we must bring some moral principles into the equation. Most forms of Christian ethics are duty-oriented, because they regard it as our highest obligation to obey the commands of God in the Bible.

We believe that an ethical decision must consider results. But a purely consequences-oriented decision-making process can't answer one key question: Which ends should we seek? As we noted in chapter 1, the results we seek often come from unconsciously held values that derive more from culture than from Scripture. The Christian worldview says that spiritual values—our relationship with God, family, unselfishness—take precedence over material ones. But we easily lose spiritual values due to subtle cultural influences—such as individualism and the desire for control. Thus uniquely Christian values can get lost when we focus only on physical health. These discussions ponder what's good for the patient without ever really considering what the word *good* means. That is, they don't consciously think through which ends are worth seeking.

In reality, rules and results shouldn't be set at odds. Rules—whether supplied by God or by society—are given because they work. But at times the results of what we know to be right might not be what we expect. In the early years of the missionary movement to central Africa, northern European Christians called to missionary service packed their belongings in a pine coffin and set sail for the tropics. They took coffins because they knew that on average Europeans lived only about one year in certain areas of interior Africa. Now from a results-oriented viewpoint, is it wise to answer God's call to missionary service in central Africa? This all depends, of course, on the value we place on physical life. Given a secularist viewpoint, since physical life is the supreme value (it's all there is, after all), a results-oriented decision-making process would say, Don't go! From a Christian perspective, however, thinking about consequences might confirm the decision to board ship. What makes the difference here isn't the question, Should you consider the results of actions? The issue is, Which ends are worth seeking? For Christians, the answer to this question arises from the Bible. The value of eternal life supersedes earthly life.

In keeping with the duty of preserving life, the right approach to curing illness might seem to be to try every medicine stocked in a pharmacy. But any wise caregiver considers the results of a drug—will it do any good? Or if you have endured the long illness of a loved one, the right thing to you might feel like unburdening yourself of this dying person. It's the result you feel you need. But biblical principle compels us to love our neighbor as ourselves and not seek selfish ends. Living according to duty and yet looking wisely to results will aim for a solution that fits everyone.

Virtues and Decision-Making

Should Christian ethics focus on decision-making? This might sound like a simple question. But some ethical views emphasize not making moral decisions but developing moral *virtues*. As we make end-of-life decisions, we are squeezed from two sides. We need internal clarity: What are my motives in this decision? But we also need to act: What am I going to do?

Virtue ethics stress *who we are* rather than *what we do*. By virtues we mean specific skills, character traits, or qualities of excellence that make up a person's inner nature. Biblical virtues include qualities like love, honesty, or faithfulness. Today, there's a renewed emphasis on ethics of character. A clear example is *The Book of Virtues: A Treasury of Great Moral Stories*, edited by former Secretary of Education, William J. Bennett.[6] As Bennett's subtitle implies, when people hear stories, they're motivated and inspired to do what's right, to commit themselves to living well. In this way, people acquire virtues.[7] Bennett doesn't seek to eliminate decision-making in favor of character development. Rather, he places decision-making in the larger context of a community of virtue—a bunch of good people thinking together will arrive at right decisions and act on them. He's right. It's important both to *know what to do* and to have the *courage to do it*. In ethics at the end of life, both of these are critical.

One drawback of virtue ethics is that its adherents don't always agree on how Christians should live. But we can't merely be good people—we need to make good decisions. When we have disagreements within a family, or between a family and doctors, we have to make a reasoned decision. Sincerity or bigheartedness or inner goodness isn't adequate.

We're squarely on the center line of the highway on this issue. We admit that ethical decision-making has too often preoccupied recent Christian ethics. The Bible, however, addresses both *doing* (making decisions) and *being* (becoming virtuous). Traditional Christians have probably merely assumed that we have the desire, courage, and character to do God's will if only we can figure out what it is. This guess is probably naïve. So we welcome the renewed emphasis on being people of inner resolve. But this doesn't by itself unravel the concrete problems we face, especially the specific questions that arise when we encounter difficult end-of-life situations.

How Can I Work Through a Moral Decision?

Considering the unique facts of a situation is important, but we need principles to guide us. Measuring results is critical, but thinking deeply about basic values is necessary. Both good character and good decision-making are essential. Is there a way to bring these insights together?

The Pieces of a Moral Act

The insights above come together when we break down a moral act into three components: (1) the actor's intention—the goal we choose in performing the act, (2) the act itself—how we achieve the goal, and (3) the results—the end we realize in the act. In a nutshell, we believe any morally right decision will measure up in all three phases.

Acts which are in themselves acceptable and which bring good results can still be wrong due to evil motives. We all know people who do good deeds to be seen by others. Likewise, we can perform sacrificial measures on behalf of a loved one to look good in front of our family or to secure our place in a will.

Similarly, actions that have good intentions and good results combined with evil means are immoral. In ethics at the end of life, for instance, someone who intends to relieve the unendurable suffering of a terminal patient and accomplishes it by smothering the patient with a pillow commits an evil act. A purely results-oriented measure of right and wrong could allow corrupt means to achieve good ends. But we say the truism "Ends don't justify means" applies.

Further, there are cases where good intentions and good means are joined to bad results. Usually, such acts are wrong. Occasionally, we judge that well-intentioned acts that turn out badly aren't evil, but good. Consider acts of heroism. A fireman running into a burning building in order to save a crying child is acting heroically even if the building collapses in flames around them both. If the attempted rescue is foolhardy because it has virtually no chance of success, we are inclined to question the moral value of the act. And in cases where the person seeking to perform the good act is well-intended but clearly negligent, we might think the act wrong. Typically, we conclude that morally right acts are those that have at least a reasonable chance of bringing good results. As we expect heroic results of medical personnel, it does us good to recognize good intentions and skillful efforts even if the results aren't what we had hoped.

So assessing moral behaviors requires looking for honorable intentions, proper means, and at least some likelihood of achieving good ends.[8] This three-part test shows that an ethical decision involves more than merely following rules. In fact, moral judgments are complex evaluations involving many factors. These factors include the three facets of a moral act, plus the facts of the situation or context in which a decision must be made, and the moral norms, principles, or rules which may be applicable.

How to Process an Ethical Decision

If a moral puzzle has this many pieces, how do we go about actually putting them together, working through an ethical decision? We offer a series of steps to walk you through a difficult moral decision.[9]

To illustrate this, let's consider a case. Mary is a vigorous young mother of three children. She is involved in a high-speed, head-on car accident. Despite heroic efforts to sustain her life, four days later the doctors tell her husband, Daniel, that she is brain-dead. The doctors start to talk about turning off the life support systems. They ask Daniel whether he would like to donate Mary's organs for transplant. She didn't have a donor card.

In a first step in responding to cases like these, *define the problem*. At this step, clear thinking requires gaining an overview of the situation and clarity on the exact question needing an answer. You might be helped by asking eight "reality-revealing" questions: What? Why? How? Who? Where? When? What are the foreseeable effects? and What are the viable alternatives?[10] In Daniel's case, the two questions are whether to agree to turning off the life support systems and whether to donate the organs. Daniel might inquire if these are the only options open to him.

Second, *probe more deeply into the problem*. Analyze the various unique factors of the situation, looking to see whether there are special extenuating circumstances. Maybe the patient gave some hint of her attitudes about extraordinary care if life ever seemed tenuous. Maybe there's an experimental surgery that doctors could perform, as much to gain valuable information about her condition as to save her life. Or maybe the patient had expressed a desire to be an organ donor. In Daniel's situation, though Mary did not have a donor card, Daniel does recall her approving of people who gave their organs so that others could live. He keeps this fact in mind as he makes his decisions.

In phase three, *carefully spell out the choices available and the consequences of each*. At this point, all who are involved in the decision look carefully at results. Exactly what will happen, as best you can discern, if you pursue this course or that course of treatment? Is there perhaps an alternative that didn't seem obvious right at first? Getting second opinions from other physicians fits in here. For Daniel, once the decision to turn off the support systems is made, the alternatives are clear: either he will donate Mary's organs or not. If he does, some people will be helped, but Mary might seem somehow diminished physically. Daniel could inquire what Mary would look like at the funeral. He might want to check to see how Mary's parents would react to organ donation.

As a fourth step, *examine relevant Bible principles*. This means reviewing the evidence for the values that seem to be driving the decision. Do they really grow out of the things that the Bible and Christianity applaud, or do they subtly emerge from a secularist or humanist culture? At this point, it's important to confer with trustworthy and knowledgeable believers, to reflect broadly on the meanings of the biblical message about life, and to give time to prayer and reflection in seeking God's direction. Daniel should consider his commitment to defending life. Discussion with his pastor might help him discern whether a refusal to turn off the life support systems and hold on to Mary is actually a human-centered desire to keep control of Mary's life. This conversation could also help him see that donating organs is a Christlike, sacrificial gift to another person.

Then, after considering all the various angles, it's time to make a decision. As a fifth step, *choose one of the options*. We recognize that this choice is sometimes ambiguous. Unfortunately, however, although the thinking process can end in indecision, life itself can't. William James points out that when a mountain climber comes to a crevasse, he has three options *for thinking*: "I can jump it," "I can't jump it," and "I don't know whether I can jump it." But he has only two options *for action*: he must either jump or not jump. Similarly, we do have to make difficult decisions at times even when the evidence leaves our thinking somewhat muddled. In this phase, Daniel simply has to decide whether to turn off the machines and whether to donate Mary's organs.

Finally, take time, if possible, *to reflect back on the decision*. It's wise, once having made the decision, to let it sit a couple of days. Sometimes, of course, this isn't possible, and we must proceed as best we can with as much dependence on God as we can muster. But if time isn't critical, a span of reflection often confirms or disconfirms the decision. This reconsideration doesn't undo everything we have already done; rather, we admit our own fallibility and give God an opportunity to correct our thinking. We know of several situations where this post-decision review prevented serious mistakes. For Daniel, spending some time with trusted family and friends reviewing the decision would be wise.

The Role of Family

The process of watching a loved one die brings out the best and worst in families. It either bonds you and builds your resolve to stand together or it makes you wish you could withdraw and hide. Working through all of these steps together as a family, however, is the best policy. Sometimes reasoning becomes difficult when people hold to diverging ideas about what to do. Steve's dilemma with Uncle Russ—see the introduction— illustrates this point perfectly. Steve wanted to *let go*, but Mary wanted to *dispose of* Uncle Russ, while Jan sought to *hold on to* him. There's no magic way to solve these questions. All you can do is talk them through honestly. Yet we do have one suggestion: You may want help working through these end-of-life decisions. Invite a trusted pastor, a sympathetic counselor, or even a wise friend to sit in on the family decision-making process. It is perfectly acceptable to ask this person not to give opinions but simply to facilitate the process. He can improve the decision-making experience by ensuring everyone is heard and everyone's interests are considered. Inviting trusted help into the process is no different than asking a lawyer to help you with legal details or a doctor to assist with the intricacies of medical treatment. Finding a clear-headed, mature person to help is a good way to solve the conflicts that often arise as you discuss complex topics.

Conclusion

The decision-making process we've shared with you moves from considering situational factors, to weighing intentions and attitudes, to spelling out actual choices and their consequences, to embracing moral principles. In considering these factors, it draws into the process all the elements of a moral choice that we sketched out above: intentions, actions, results, situational factors, and relevant principles. After evaluating all these matters, a family can in prayer offer its decision to the Lord and humbly act as it has decided is right. Sometimes this is uncomplicated. Sometimes it plunges us into seemingly unresolvable quandaries. Yet we can depend on what God says in the Bible, the leading of God's Spirit, and the consensus of God's people as we seek answers that allow us to live out genuine Christian values.

This discussion lays important elements of a Christian ethic, and it turns out that decision-making is far more complicated than simply following rules. Rules exist to protect our most basic values. This means that any effort that seeks to protect life will build on a clear understanding of what human life is. So how should we view life? What does the Bible teach us about the value and nature of human life?

three

What Is the Meaning of Human Life?

Within a month, a major news magazine ran two cover stories on violence.[1] One story, focusing on youthful gunslingers in Omaha, quotes a twenty-year veteran police officer: "This particular generation of kids has absolutely no value for human life. They don't know what it is to die or what it means to pull the trigger."[2]

These youth cherish neither others' lives nor, apparently, even their own.

Other people place great value on all life indiscriminately. For example, the former executive director of the Sierra Club, David Brown, says, "While the death of young men in war is unfortunate, it is no more serious than [the] touching of mountains and wilderness areas by humankind."[3] Similarly, the president of People for the Ethical Treatment of Animals, Ingrid Newkirk, writes, "A rat is a pig is a dog is a boy."[4]

In the face of losing a loved one, we feel immediate outrage at such cheapening of human life. But what does it really mean that human life has special value?

How Can I View Human Life?

One dreadful day last spring, I (David) went with Sandy, my wife, to two funerals. One family had lost a devoted dad who'd delighted his family and greatly honored God. The other family had lost a cantankerous father who'd bullied his wife, browbeat his family, and menaced his business associates. If you've ever lost a loved one, it probably brought an unbearable sadness. But if you've ever known someone who'd become a burden, his passing probably brought relief.

Regardless of whether we value an individual emotionally or sentimentally, it remains true that all persons have value before God. Knowing this might cause someone freed by the passing of a troublesome person to feel guilty for experiencing relief, so we feel compelled to say this: Loving a person who is hard to love involves a difficult commitment. God honors that faithful service. But there's nothing wrong with feeling thankful when, in God's good time, that period of difficult service is over.

Even when we have a family member who is hard to love emotionally, that person's value lies deeper. Respecting that person is still morally honorable. Good, bad, or curmudgeon through and through, each human being has inestimable value.

The Image of God

Christians look to the Bible to understand the true meaning of human life, and a biblical view of humanness begins back at the beginning of human history. The Old Testament tantalizes us with only a few brief references to the *image of God*. The creation account in the first chapters of the Bible reads simply, "Then God said, 'Let us make man in our image, in our likeness.' . . . So God created man in his own image, in the image of God he created him; male and female he created them" (Genesis 1:26–27). This beautiful text is easy to appreciate but more difficult to understand. But what we can know for sure is that a boy is not a rat; nor is he a pig or a dog. Only he and all other humans, out of all creation, bear the image of the Creator.

Bold Insights on God's Image

Some theologians have said that the image of God refers to a particular quality that human beings possess, say, the ability to think. Others have claimed that it means an activity, like ruling the earth. Recent evidence suggests that the word *image* implies a richer, more animated appreciation for human life. The *image* likely refers not to one particular quality but to who we are in all our fullness. "According to Genesis 1," one scholar writes, "a man does not have the image of God, nor is he made in the image of God, but is himself the image of God." God didn't create us *in* his image; he created us *as* his image. The image of God isn't just something we *have* or *do*; it's something we *are*. To be human is to be the image of God, the representative of the Creator.[5]

Human Life Is Created

What a strange creation we are! We are at once frail, unique, broken, and redeemed.

We are frail. In one sense, we *stand with* the rest of creation—the rocks, the plants, and the animals. As part of the created order, we're subject to the lordship of the Creator. We're made of dust. This suggests both the connection of our bodies to the physical world and, at one level, the frailty, limitation, and insignificance of our lives (Genesis 3:19; 18:27; Psalm 103:14).

We are unique. On the other hand, because we're uniquely created as the image of God, we *stand apart* from the rest of creation. Of all creation, it is only of humans that God says, "Let us make . . . in our image." After creating Adam and Eve, God says creation is *very* good (Genesis 1:31). God grants us dominion over the rest of creation (Genesis 1:28–30; 9:1–2; Psalm 8:4–9). Thus, while we share with all creation our "created-ness," we alone occupy a special relationship to the Creator. The view that humans arose from nowhere and are headed nowhere is false. Rather, as the psalmist wrote, we are "fearfully and wonderfully made" (Psalm 139:14). Humans are precious to God because we bear God's image.

We are broken. Despite this incredible privilege of being near to God, the first couple rebelled. They fell into the temptation to become like God. In open disobedience to the Creator, they tried to rise above their created state. Instead of becoming "as God,"[6] however, they broke their personal relationship with the Creator and suffered banishment from the Garden.

And throughout the Bible we see a fourth truth unfold: *We are redeemed.* As a result of Adam and Eve's choices, sin entered the world. Alienation, insecurity, war, sickness, and death still plague us. The scarred humans we see around us are hardly an adequate model for a study of "human life created as the image of God." Yet, though tarnished, the image is still a reality. Due to sin, we're unable in our own strength to regain fellowship with God. But God can rescue us. Because we're created as his image, God offers to rescue us by offering a covenant relationship with him. This relationship is available through Jesus Christ, and it leads to God's renewing his image in us.

Human Life Is Personal

Most adults have had the experience of entering the presence of a dying loved one and feeling he or she "isn't really there." Even so, that person's being fully human doesn't stop until life stops. A human being who hangs between life and death has as much inherent value—and remains just as much a person—as the people who stand around the deathbed.

Picture these things about your loved one. As a creation of God who bears his image, each human being is a member of the human family. God knows us and watches over us at every stage of life. A human person—in fact or at least potentially—has an ability to be aware of self, to relate to natural surroundings, and to relate, often very imperfectly, to other persons and to God. The earthly life of a person begins at conception and ceases when these characteristics and abilities, either actual or potential, come to an end.[7]

In speaking this way, we don't want to separate the concepts *human* and *person.* We think it's wrong to say that some organisms (say, unborn children or comatose patients) are human, but not persons—and therefore of lower worth or status than fully personal humans. An individual doesn't earn or attain human status by gaining or possessing certain abilities such as the ability to think. He doesn't lose it if he slips below a certain level of intelligence, mobility, or consciousness. The value of human life is rooted in who we are, not in what we do. The beloved seventy-two-year-old grandmother battling cancer and the nineteen-year-old man paralyzed when he drove drunk have the same worth as the doctor who works on them or the pastor who calls on them. As a human person, your loved one, made by God to be his representative, however saintly or sinful, whole or limited, is of worth simply by virtue of his or her status as a member of the human family.[8] The dying patient able to *think* less or *move* less is not *worth* less.

This intrinsic value of human beings is what makes murder so wrong, whether it happens at the hands of a mugger or a misguided pro-euthanasia doctor. By equating a life for a life—and no more than a life for a life, and only the life of the murderer—the Bible assumes the equal and essential worth of each person. Genesis 9:6 boldly says that taking a person's life is wrong because all people enjoy a divine-like status. As Walter Kaiser notes, "To kill a person was tantamount to killing God in effigy."[9] To take a person's life, then, violates the sanctity of one who is in some respect like her Creator.

This doesn't imply, Christians recognize, that we're morally worthy in the sense that we deserve salvation. We are broken. We don't earn God's favor in any way. Our good works don't make us acceptable to God (Ephesians 2:8–9). Yet we're of inestimable value. For example, my newborn niece, Kama, three days old as I write, is powerless to earn her parents' affection or care. Kama's parents highly value her—and so do we—not because of what she can do or the fact that she doesn't yet quarrel with her siblings, but because of who she is. Similarly, because all humans are of intrinsic worth, all deserve our respect and protection regardless of their abilities,[10] because each one is the image of God.

How Are Sanctity of Life and Quality of Life Important?

People weighing the value of human life often pit the ideas *sanctity of life* and *quality of life* against each other. Unfortunately, these expressions sometimes devolve into slogans in a political debate. *Sanctity of life* is the key phrase for *pro-life* supporters, while *pro-choice* defenders rally behind *quality of life*. To make sense of caring for a loved one, however, we need to move beyond slogans.

Sanctity of Life

Taken literally, *sanctity of life* could imply *life* is in itself something holy or sacred, set apart—in some sense, like God himself. But in a more precise usage, *sanctity* emphasizes the claim that a human life in its totality—as a physical/spiritual whole—has deep spiritual meaning. God wants us to live and breathe—and rescues us from sin—so we can enjoy a covenant relationship of love with him. Because people have inestimable value, we have a duty to preserve their lives. If I see a man drowning in water, I ought to help him to safety if I can. If I see a man "drowning" in a sea of bacteria from an infected appendix, I have a duty to help him to better health. Morally, there's little to be distinguished. When medicine provides a reasonable chance for sustained or improved health, we have a responsibility to give treatment and to accept it. Our responsibility is to "seek only what's good" for the patient, the well-founded principle of *beneficence* (see chapter 1).

If *sanctity* refers to the spiritual significance of human life, to what does the word *life* point? Some people think that the sanctity of life principle means that *physical* life is in itself sacred and set apart by God. This implies to some that a pro-life position requires us to be pro-*physical* life. This notion is noble and honorable in its intentions, but simplistic in its understanding of both theological and medical realities.

If *sanctity of life* means the sanctity of mere *physical* life, then a pro-life stance suggests that we continue treatment of living bodies even after we know our efforts are medically futile. Clinically, this is total treatment—prolonging merely physical life regardless of the costs, even against the wishes of the recipient. In such cases, we believe that our efforts amount to prolonging death rather than extending life. This attitude is *holding on* as Jan wanted to do with Uncle Russ—the never-ceasing, futile attempt, at all costs, to try to save the dying from their death.[11] It sees physical death as the ultimate evil, so paying any amount to defeat it is well worth the cost. In reality, this view is arrogant. Far from seeking to value what God values, it presumes we have ultimate control over life and death. Not only does this attitude deny the reality of death, but it diminishes a full appreciation for life's true worth.

A view that hallows physical life confuses biological life with human life. Here's why: while biological life is *essential* to the image of God, it's not *sufficient* for the image. Your loved one is more than an interrelated collection of physiologically functioning human organs. It's not mere physical life but human life in all its fullness—including the physical, personal, and spiritual dimensions—that is sacred. It's as a member of humankind, as a person who naturally possesses certain capacities, characteristics, and interests, that each human being has value.

You may wonder if this distinction strengthens the arguments of radical proponents of euthanasia. One euthanasia advocate, James Rachels, indeed separates *biological* life and *biographical* life. Biographical life refers to life a person chooses, experiences, and lives, as over and against the physical functioning of the body. Using this contrast, Rachels argues that biological life has no inherent value. Meaning, he says, comes from biographical life. In his view, a person has an unlimited right to give up physical life whenever his biographical life stops having the meaning he wishes it to have.[12] In contrast, we argue that the physical and spiritual life of a person seen as a whole is valuable. Biographical life, which is important, assumes the physical life God has given also has high value.

Our perspective differs, therefore, both from Rachels and from a naïve extend-life-at-all-costs view. Champions of euthanasia place all the value in *biographical* life—which implies that there's no inherent significance to the physical. This is why they claim absolute control over the ending of human life. But a poorly thought-out pro-life view assigns nearly infinite worth to *biological* life—which implies that the spiritual and psychological are meaningless. It requires us to keep bodies alive as long as possible. In a strange way this also amounts to a claim of absolute control. In essence, this inadequate pro-life view says, "Physical life is supremely valuable;

we can never let go." This plays down God's right to take life in his good timing. Of course, the radical euthanasia perspective declares, "Physical life is mine; I'll take it if I choose." This, too, cuts God out.

Few Christian thinkers supported the sanctity of human life more strongly than Karl Barth. Yet he came to realize that *holding on*, a position he held earlier in life, is unsound: "The question also arises whether this kind of artificial prolongation of life does not amount to human arrogance in the opposite direction, whether the fulfillment of medical duty does not threaten to become fanaticism, reason folly, and the required assisting of human life a forbidden torturing of it. A case is at least conceivable in which a doctor might have to recoil from this prolongation of life no less than from its arbitrary shortening."[13] Barth recognized that letting life "expire under our watch" is different from seeking death. Holding on to life can be as arrogant as taking it. God is in charge of death as he is of life. A time comes when attempts to prolong life are pointless, and to deny what God is doing when he takes a life is as blasphemous as taking it without good reason.

Quality of Life

In the past, proponents of euthanasia defended the practice in cases of unrelieved physical pain. Now it's possible to control most pain quite adequately.[14] Thus, defenders of euthanasia have expanded their use of the word *pain* to include any undesirable side effects of medical technology, loss of dignity and self-determination, or a decreased quality of life. Consequently, some speak today of a *quality of life* below which life isn't worth living or sustaining.

The quality of life principle has been part of medical

practice since the days of Hippocrates. Quality of life is critical in medicine, because doctors must predict the quality of life that could result from any treatment decision. If open heart surgery, for instance, will so weaken an aged patient that she will never get out of bed, the quality of life principle tells the medical staff to forego the bypass surgery in favor of a less aggressive strategy. If another round of chemotherapy will kill a patient, doctors choose to discontinue treatment—which should seem obvious. But when our emotions overtake us in fighting for the life of a loved one, we sometimes push for more treatment that actually harms. Good medicine starts by accepting the intrinsic value of patients. Good medicine then also considers the patient's quality of life—not to decide whether a patient should continue to live but to determine how best to treat.

Today's proponents of euthanasia, however, don't endorse using the quality of a person's life as a guide to choosing between treatment options. In certain cases, they urge us to use it as the yardstick for deciding whether life has value at all. They reason that if the quality of a loved one's life doesn't measure up to some minimum standard, we needn't support his life at all. The right to life, this view implies, is something a patient earns by virtue of possessing the ability to do certain things or to enjoy certain experiences.

This use of the quality of life principle ignores the more foundational principle, the sanctity of life. Suppose doctors begin forming therapeutic decisions on the basis of the quality of a person's life apart from considering the basic sanctity of that life. It isn't a leap at all to see how they could sacrifice human life in the name of other values, whether economic or cultural or personal.

By misusing the quality of life principle in this way,

for example, a person may logically decide that it's more merciful to starve a Down's syndrome infant born with a closed esophagus than to perform surgery. We say *logically* because this judgment follows deductively from certain assumptions. If it really is better for a Down's infant not to live at all than to live a life that's in some sense of lesser quality, then the choice is quite logical. If peak human self-fulfillment is more important than life itself, then the decision is logical. Taking the infant's perspective, however, we have to wonder whether she would ever really choose nonexistence over life. Even if the life of the Down's syndrome child is somehow of lesser quality when it's compared to the other family members—and we wouldn't at all argue that—a quality of life appropriate to her is still possible.

From the viewpoint of parents who are thinking self-centeredly of their own lives, of course, letting a Down's syndrome baby die might seen better than rearing the child. Without a fundamental commitment to the significance of that child's life, the social, economic, and emotional implications of living with a handicapped child seem overwhelming. Again, however, the fact that the Down's syndrome infant will never be able to enjoy Shakespeare in the same way English professors might doesn't mean she shouldn't live. In short, the quality of life principle can help decide the relative merit of different treatment options, but not the fundamental value of a person's life.

What Are the Implications for Life's Meaning?

With this understanding about human life—that God creates all persons as his image, authorizes them to represent him, and affirms their intrinsic worth—we're prepared to address several practical results of our personhood.

Ownership of Life

Suppose John tries to pressure Susan to make an important decision about her life, and Susan doesn't agree with John's views. If Susan is typical, she might say, "Whose life is it, anyway?" In this retort, Susan implies that her life is *hers*. If she means a relative autonomy (and not an absolute independence from God), then her answer is rightly assertive. This raises interesting questions about who "owns" our lives and about how this ownership affects the way we should live.

The Christian worldview teaches that we live in this world by grace. All we have comes to us from the hand of a loving God as a gift to be cherished and shared, never possessed or clutched. Life itself is one of those gifts, given to us to enjoy fully and use wisely. We don't own our lives, however, because life itself comes from the Creator, and what God creates, he owns. The psalmist expresses the significance of this truth: "The earth is the Lord's, and everything in it, the world, and all who live in it" (Psalm 24:1). Job recognizes this as he stands in the midst of ruin and proclaims, "The Lord gave and the Lord has taken away" (Job 1:21). Jesus teaches this same principle in instructing the Pharisees to "give to Caesar what is Caesar's, and to God what is God's" (Matthew 22:21). Whatever bears the image of the king belongs to the king; whatever bears the image of God belongs to God.

When we acknowledge God as the rightful owner of all he creates, including our lives, we recognize that God has an authority which rightfully surpasses ours. All of us are stewards of our own lives. We have an obligation to take into account the One who has entrusted that life to us—to care for it and nurture it under his watchful and gracious eye. We recognize that God knows what's best for us even when we don't comprehend his ways.

This basic reality suggests that when we choose to take a human life through suicide or through active euthanasia, we usurp authority for a decision that isn't ours. We express not an appropriate relative self-rule, but an absolute independence by rebelling against God. By choosing death for ourselves or a loved one, we're also implying that God isn't trustworthy—that he doesn't know what he's doing in giving us life and allowing us to experience difficult times. In such acts, we destroy something that doesn't belong to us. We violate our trusteeship and defraud the owner.

Life As a Gift

Life is our most precious possession. It's the good without which no other good is possible. Christians understand that life is a gift from a loving and caring God. From this perspective, to choose death rather than life is an unconscionable expression of ingratitude to the Giver of life. Ramsey puts this well:

> "The immorality of choosing death as an end is founded upon our religious faith that life is a *gift*. A gift is not given if it is not received as a gift, no more than a gift can be given out of anything other than kindness or generosity (to give out of flattery or duplicity or to curry favor is not a gift). To choose death as an end is to throw the gift back in the face of the Giver; it would be to defeat his gift-giving."[15]

Gratitude is the only appropriate response to a gift of great value. We show our gratitude not only in what we say about the gift but also in what we do with it. For example, if my colleague gives me a rare edition of John Calvin's theological classic *The Institutes of Christian Religion*, and I tell him I'm immensely grateful for his gift but turn around and donate it to the Boy Scout paper drive, I commit an unscrupulous act. Not only do I waste a valuable book, I show utter disrespect for the one who gave me the valued gift and who rightfully expects my gratitude.

Some might argue that if something is really given as a gift, it becomes the property of the one who receives the gift to do with as he or she pleases. Otherwise, what we call a gift is really a loan. But such reasoning cuts off the precious act of gift-giving from its context of relationship. How I treat my gift reflects how I regard its giver. If I toss away the rare book, I tear a relationship with my colleague. By my actions I say in effect, "I don't value what you value. I will decide what has value for me." I show my disregard for his feelings and for our relationship.

How much more is this the case when the gift and the Giver are more clearly connected as when an all-wise and all-loving God gives me the gift of my very life! If I show wanton disregard for this gift (if I decide to end my life because I believe I have the right to do so), I show blasphemous disrespect toward the One who gave it. Thus, choosing death is to say, "God, I have the right to choose what's best for me. Life has the value I assign it, not the value its Maker declares." This is an act of ingratitude toward the One who's working to accomplish good in my life. It's throwing God's gift of life back in his face.

Conclusion

Defining the nature of human life is as difficult as it is crucial. Obviously, not everyone assumes the basic value of human life. For Christians, however, human life is meaningful because of its status as a creation of God—in his image. The next question concerns the end of human life. Evolutionists may think of a human death as a minor event in the ageless struggle for biological survival. Skeptics may see it as a tragic but predictable end to personal existence. We may be uncertain exactly what it means in the case of our loved one. So how do Christians view human death?

four

What Is Human Death?

"Death makes equal the high and the low."[1] It's the experience of peasant and prince, of bag lady and billionaire. It's that constant and unavoidable reminder that our existence is limited. Death is the appointment no one escapes, a mystery that both fascinates and horrifies. We know we can't avoid death forever.

Death is all around us, reminding us that, one day, we too shall succumb to its insatiable appetite. But because of its uncertainties, we build barriers that shield it from view. Our culture distances us from real death. We see it on TV—violent deaths, comic deaths, emergency room deaths. A staff doctor yells "Call it!" and a colleague looks at her watch and says the time. It feels absurd, like a referee calling time at a football game. When it comes down to it, few of us know what happens in the moments (or months) when a loved one hangs between life and death. *What* happens? We know that in some cases the fact that death has come isn't at all clear. How do we know *when* it happens?

And while we all will share in this common experience, we don't agree on its significance. The Christian, who understands human life to be the creation of a morally good God, views death as the end of our earthly life and our passage into God's presence. The New Ager agrees that death is an entrance to another life, but she thinks this means reincarnation. The humanist, for example, whose worldview is directed by a secular mentality, sees death as the absolute end of human existence. Death is a brick wall, not a door to another life.

What Does the Bible Teach Me About Death?

At the outset, we want to know how the biblical authors understood death. Defining *death* is important. Clarity here will help us understand the limits of our obligation to respond to terminal situations.

Three Meanings of the Word "Death"

The word "death" has several uses. First, the Bible obviously uses the term "death" for *physical death*. Death is a destructive force; "my tent is destroyed" (Jeremiah 10:20). Death is when the spiritual self or soul,[2] the non-physical aspect of the person, separates from the body. The writer of Ecclesiastes says, "The dust returns to the ground it came from, and the spirit returns to God who gave it" (12:7). The apostle James wrote, "The body without the spirit is dead" (2:26).

Looking back in history, many Greeks disliked the body. But the biblical view sees soul and body in close interaction. Biblical writers assumed that in death, the spiritual self leaves the body. The body decomposes and returns to the earth while the soul returns to its Giver. Death marks the transition from one mode or state to another form of existence, but not to extinction.[3] The Bible implies that the soul can exist in the next life without a body, but it's essentially incomplete in that form. Although death disrupts the unity of a person for a time, this disunity is not forever. At the final resurrection, the body and soul are reunited (1 Corinthians 15:35–58).

Second, the Bible uses death to speak of a person's spiritual relation to God. Death in this sense is *spiritual death*. Spiritual death describes a broken relationship with God that results from the human family's fallen nature in Adam (Romans 5:12–14). As a result of sin, we're hostile toward God and alienated from him (Genesis 2:17; Romans 6:23). Spiritual death means we have no capacity or desire for moving toward a relationship with God (Ephesians 2:1–2).

The Good News of the Bible is that spiritual death needn't be our final state. God can make alive anyone who is dead in sin. Anyone who is spiritually dead can have new birth in Christ (1 John 3:14). Life, in this sense, is eternal life—life lived, starting now and stretching into eternity, in an intimate relationship with God. Eternal life is, at its core, a covenant relationship with God. The Good News is that for those who have been born anew and are alive in Christ, physical death is a door to a new and deeper experience of the presence of God.

The bad news for the unbeliever is that in addition to the damage of physical death itself—the loss of physical life and the end of personal relationships in this life—there remains no further possibility for spiritual life. This predicament is the logical outcome for the person who experiences physical death while being spiritually dead. The Bible calls this "eternal death" or the "second death." *Eternal death* is a third, metaphorical use of death. This phrase refers to the final state of separation from God. All opportunity for spiritual life is past for those who die in this condition; they will experience eternal alienation from God. So death isn't the end of existence. In eternal death, unbelievers won't be left to an eternal slumber in peace or nonexistence. They experience punishment for their disobedience and unbelief in the form of eternal separation from God and all his goodness (Matthew 25:46; 2 Thessalonians 1:9).

Death As Unnatural

We hear people say, "Death is a natural part of life." In *My Name Is Asher Lev*, novelist Chaim Potok recounts how he came to understand the mystery of life and death when he and his father came upon a dead bird on the side of the street.

> "Is it dead, Papa?" I was six and could not bring myself to look at it.
> "Yes," I heard him say in a sad and distant way.
> "Why did it die?"
> "Everything that lives must die."
> "Everything?"
> "Yes."

"You, too, Papa? And Mama?"

"Yes."

"And me?"

"Yes," he said. Then he added in Yiddish, "But may it be only after you live a long and good life, my Asher." I could not grasp it. I forced myself to look at the bird. Everything alive would one day be as still as that bird?

"Why?" I asked.

"That's the way the Ribbono Shel Olom made His world, Asher."

"Why?"

"So life would be precious, Asher. Something that is yours forever is never precious."

"I'm frightened, Papa."

"Come. We'll go home and have our Shabbos meal and sing zemiros to the Ribbono Shel Olom."[4]

Life is precious indeed. This makes death a painful loss. Some people, though, try to find comfort by claiming that death is "natural." They find the sense of participating in the great cycle of life and death to be a great consolation. New Age enthusiasts, who adopt forms of alternative medicine, tend to see death as natural. "We live, we die," they will say. "Our bodies nourish the next generation. We're connected to the eternal process of cosmic life!"

But is death really natural? Is it really as normal as the rainstorms that break up the monotony of sunny weather? The Bible says that death intrudes on our original makeup as God imagers—what he intended for us when he made us. It's alien, foreign. In contrast to the great cycle of life concept, the Bible sees death as the ultimate invader, a destructive menace. It appears that the Creator didn't intend death as part of human experience. God did create our first parents with a capacity to die. Perhaps, though, if there had been no rebellion against God, they wouldn't have died at all. But in fact, sin entered the human family as a result of Adam and Eve's disobedience to God's command. According to the Bible, this is the origin of human death.[5]

Death is an intrusion into a creation God regarded as "very good" (Genesis 1:31). Death doesn't come as a friend. It's an enemy, for it not only puts an end to physical life and the relationships we cherish, it can seal a person's eternal destiny (1 Corinthians 15:26). At the same time, for those who have new life in Christ, death is a *conquered* enemy. While we must all experience death (God doesn't reverse the course of history), the "sting of death," its ultimate power to destroy forever, is removed for the believer (1 Corinthians 15:54–57). Because Christ died for us, the power of death has been extinguished. Eternal life with God, a covenant relationship with the Creator, awaits those who trust in God (Galatians 3:13; Isaiah 25:8).

How Does Your Physician Think About Death?

In order to make wise end-of-life decisions, however, we also have to think about how medicine understands death. To do that we have to clarify what physical death is.[6]

Defining Death

In the past, of course, it was easy to tell when someone was dead. If a body had no pulse and didn't breathe, it was dead. Today, in an era of advanced medical technology, these issues aren't so simple.[7] Using life support systems, physicians can keep a patient's heart beating and lungs breathing even though the brain is dead. (Once brain cells die, they can't be resuscitated short of a back-from-the-dead type miracle. Central nervous system cells don't regenerate or repair themselves as do other cells.) The invention of life support systems thus made it necessary to understand death in a new way.

Defining death is primarily the task of theology and philosophy. When Christians study what humans are, they start by thinking about how humans exhibit the image of God. Once theology establishes a suitable definition of death, it's right to consider clues by which the *diagnosis* of death can be made. Establishing the criteria for diagnosing death may involve the cooperation of theology, but it is primarily the job of science. So medical science establishes uniform tests that tell us when the criteria for death have been met. Armed with these criteria and tests, a physician can go to the bedside and confirm a diagnosis of death.

It is most straightforward to think of physical death as the permanent cessation of functioning of the body as a whole. The phrase "as a whole" implies going beyond the traditional heart and lung approach. It includes brain death and recognizes that the body lives physically when its various systems are integrated and supporting each other. This reflects a better understanding of what really happens as the body shuts down during the dying process, and it takes account of the shortcoming of traditional understandings, which ignored brain death.

But this improvement still doesn't completely answer our theological concern—that the right definition of death has to say something about the spiritual event that takes place. Yet if we keep in mind that the phrase "as a whole" includes the spiritual dimension of the person, then we have a starting point for a good definition. So we define *physical death* in this way: *death is the permanent cessation of integrated functioning of a human person, which makes the body incapable of sustaining a living soul.* This definition includes both the breakdown of the physical life processes and the separation of the spiritual self from the body. If we exclude the spiritual side of this definition, we would reduce the human person to a physical entity.[8]

Diagnosing Death

Now that we have a definition of death, we can discuss how to identify that death has occurred. To do this, doctors must check certain clearly observable facts. Traditionally, physicians made diagnoses of death through the use of simple, time-honored bedside skills. They documented the absence of vital signs: heart sound, pulse, and respiration.[9] But in the late 1950s, French neurologists recognized that they could maintain on respirators certain brain-damaged patients who were in a far more profound state of unconsciousness. These patients were entirely unresponsive and significantly different from any comatose patients previously seen. Even though machines kept them "alive," their condition appeared consistent with death. The neurologists called this state *coma depasse*.[10]

Other physicians soon recognized the same condition. Obviously, doctors needed to know whether such individuals with completely destroyed brains are alive or dead. So an ad hoc committee of the Harvard Medical School gathered in 1968 to establish new criteria for death in light of *coma depasse*. The committee recognized that the brain regulates all other organs, sustains all conscious human life, and maintains the integration of the whole person. The committee decided, therefore, that if a patient's brain could no longer function, a physician could declare that person dead even though heart and lung activity continued to function by means of artificial support. The committee proposed four criteria for diagnosing brain death.

1. "Unreceptivity and unresponsivity": the patient is entirely unaware of his environment and unable to respond to "externally applied stimuli and inner need."

2. No movements or breathing: the patient shows no evidence of spontaneous muscle movement or respiration for a period of one hour.

3. No reflexes: the patient's fixed, dilated pupils provide the best evidence; other reflex centers also show no response.

4. Flat electroencephalogram: the patient's flat EEG is "of great confirmatory value" in diagnosing an absence of biological activity of upper brain cells. This evaluation is to be repeated twenty-four hours later, and if there's no change in the results, the diagnosis stands.[11]

Initially, as we might expect, some opposed diagnosing death by these new criteria. However, over a relatively short period of time, the so-called Harvard criteria became widely accepted. It soon became the prevailing view that "persons who have died need not have 'life'-sustaining measures inflicted upon their unburied corpses, needlessly and at great expense to their families."[12]

Since 1968, physicians have made some modifications to the Harvard criteria (they deleted criterion four). But by and large, the medical community now accepts them. These indicators form a reasonable basis for diagnosing clinical death. The criteria recognize that a human is an integral whole, so that when the brain is irreversibly no longer functioning (even though other organs are sustained artificially), a human being has ceased to exist in this life. Use of these indicators is consistent, in our view, with the biblical understanding of human death as the cessation of physical function and the release of the soul into the next life.

In 1981, the President's Commission report, *Defining Death*, proposed an updated version.[13] Today doctors look for these indicators when they diagnose death in respirator-dependent patients. The criteria have stood the ultimate tests: the test of clinical accuracy and the test of time. Thus physicians use two separate and equal tests to determine death: cessation of cardiopulmonary function when respirators aren't involved, and whole brain failure when respirators are involved. In both situations, the doctor must make a determination of death in accord with accepted medical standards.[14]

Death is a multifaceted event. Our definition recognizes this. Above all, the death of the brain is what clearly indicates final physical death. Other organ failures will result by necessity if the brain dies. Armed with these indicators, based on the understanding that a death of a human person is cessation of the organism as a physical and spiritual whole, a clinician can make the diagnosis of death with accuracy.

Persistent Vegetative State

Since 1968, further developments have complicated our understanding of death. It is now possible to maintain a body when the individual has no potential whatsoever to regain conscious life of any kind, even though part of the brain still functions. We now call this condition the *persistent vegetative state* (PVS).[15] Like brain death, the possibility of PVS arose because of medical technological advances. Prior to respirator support, clinicians didn't think about whole brain death. Prior to more sophisticated life support and resuscitative techniques, they didn't consider the possibility of PVS. The legal battle surrounding the care of Karen Ann Quinlan, who remained unconscious in PVS for eleven years before dying naturally, brought PVS out into the open.[16]

In essence, PVS is *upper brain death*. Roughly, the brain has two major sections, the upper brain (called the neocortex) and the lower brain (the brain stem). The upper brain is responsible for all conscious life and therefore is necessary to sustain personal human life as we know and value it. The lower brain regulates certain physical functions like breathing, heartbeat, digestion, and some muscle movements. PVS individuals have irretrievably lost all upper brain function and therefore have no hope of regaining consciousness or reintegrating themselves. In such individuals, however, the lower brain can continue to maintain the heart and lungs without a respirator. Thus, when life support is turned off, the PVS patient may not die. But the patient has no hope for awareness of any kind. This is what happened to Karen Ann Quinlan.

It's easy to confuse the terms "brain death," "PVS," and "coma." Brain death occurs when the entire brain is destroyed. So-called "pulling the plug" of such a patient does not end the patient's life. A brain-dead patient is already dead. Life support systems are discontinued in recognition of this fact, and we believe that this is a morally right decision. In fact, in many states, it's the law.

PVS is diagnosed only when there is complete damage to the *upper* brain, so that conscious life is forever impossible. But with a functioning lower brain, a PVS patient can breathe without a respirator. If it is fed and cared for, a body can function in this state for many years.

Coma, on the other hand, is an altered state of consciousness that occurs because of severe brain dysfunction. A comatose person is unaware of self and environment even when the body is stimulated externally. He or she seems asleep and doesn't respond to the environment. But there's an important difference between coma and PVS. Some coma patients recover full consciousness with no loss of function. Others experience partial recovery with various degrees of limitation. Still others may decline from coma to PVS or directly into death. This depends on the degree, location, and cause of the damage to the brain. But unlike a PVS patient, some comatose patients regain consciousness and enjoy a relationship with God and other people.

One helpful warning: Although patients who aren't responding may seem to be completely unaware of their environment, they sometimes hear and remember what is said in their presence. Many pastors know of cases where people said things when they thought the patient could not hear. Obviously this can later cause problems. Families should keep this reality in mind as they discuss sensitive subjects.

What Is the Status of PVS Patients?

What should we say about the status of PVS patients? Are they alive? We argued that human life was created by God as his image to serve as his representatives (see chapter 3). The image of God requires that persons have certain capacities—at least potentially—if they are to represent him in this life. As we employ these abilities, we carry out God's purpose for us. A functioning upper brain is necessary if an individual is to exercise the godlike qualities with which his Creator fashioned him. It seems, therefore, that the irreversible loss of upper brain function places an individual beyond the capacity of responding to God and imaging him. A potentially functional upper brain, it seems, is necessary to live out the image of God, and it appears that physical function of heart and lungs isn't by itself sufficient for the continuation of God's image.

What should we do? By maintaining the physical life of PVS patients, are we maintaining "living cadavers"? Does ceasing to maintain their physical lives amount to taking a human life? It's tempting to conclude that sustaining a Karen Ann Quinlan—with no hope whatever for any conscious awareness—is maintaining a "living cadaver," and that ceasing to support her body isn't ending a human life.[17]

We need to know more about PVS before we can confidently reach such a conclusion. At present, PVS is a clinical diagnosis. It's not always possible to know for certain that total upper brain death has occurred. In fact, some clinical diagnoses are proved wrong at autopsy. But even if we could detect when the upper brain is completely dead, we aren't sure even then that this individual no longer is a God imager. Theologians and philosophers must continue to address the question—if we don't, the courts (which aren't adequately prepared to deal with these issues but are more than ready to make pronouncements) will respond.[18]

This means that there's a clinical condition that's halfway between total brain death and coma. It's clear to us that total brain death means a patient no longer need be sustained artificially. Similarly, it's obvious that comatose patients should be sustained. But PVS challenges all of these: our definition of death, our traditional understanding of the image of God, and our reflex to care for the dying. With a full grasp of the weightiness of a situation that may involve your loved one, we're inclined *not to require artificial sustenance of properly diagnosed PVS patients*. But until this matter is addressed more fully, we continue to ponder its significance.

Conclusion

Although at first blush the meaning of death may seem obvious, stepping closer to the issue shows that this question is really quite difficult. We argued that an understanding of human life should focus on some capacity to image God, not merely on minimal biological function. Just as perplexing is deciding how the discussion up to this point applies specifically to euthanasia. So we now ask: How should we assess various strategies for responding to end-of-life ethical dilemmas? Is euthanasia morally appropriate, or are there better alternatives?

five

Why Reject Euthanasia?

Late one evening a news program reported the words of a prosecutor discussing a case involving yet another physician-assisted suicide (PAS). The district attorney had worked to convict Dr. Kevorkian of breaking a Michigan law. Yet this prosecutor, whose job is to uphold the law, told the reporter that he believed the physician had done a morally right act. The district attorney prosecuted, he said, only because he felt duty-bound to uphold Michigan law. But he personally agreed with the doctor. It's morally right, he said, for physicians to help their patients commit suicide. He hoped that the laws of his state would change to reflect this idea.

How Are Attitudes Toward Euthanasia Changing?

Evidence of attitude change is all around us. The former governor of Colorado Richard Lamm reportedly told some senior citizens, "You've got a duty to die and get out of the way. Let the other society, our kids, build a reasonable life."[1] His remarks brought howls of protest. Yet some consider his words prophetic. Public perceptions about the permissibility of doctors' killing their patients appear to be shifting. The Hemlock Society, a group dedicated to legalizing PAS, published Derek Humphry's *Final Exit* in 1985.[2] The manual gives detailed instructions on how suffering persons can quietly and successfully end their lives. The book quickly climbed bestseller lists, and many hailed it as "much needed" and "long overdue."

In 1988 the *Journal of the American Medical Association* published a provocative, milestone essay entitled "It's Over, Debbie." In it, an anonymous resident-physician told how he had given a lethal dose of morphine to a terminal cancer patient who died soon after. He said he wanted to relieve her suffering. The surprise isn't that the event took place, nor that *JAMA* reported it. The real shock was that so many readers supported the resident's action. *JAMA*'s editor, Dr. George E. Lundberg, comments, "The response from the public suggests that many of our patients would want active euthanasia if needed, and they would want it performed by doctors."[3]

"When we have statutes on the books permitting lawful physician aid-in-dying for the terminally ill," writes Derek Humphry, "I believe that along with this reform there will come a more tolerant attitude toward other exceptional cases."[4] The first of these statutes is

79

now in place. Oregon has legalized PAS, and several other states are preparing legislation to legalize the practice. Though the United States Supreme Court unanimously ruled in June 1997 that individuals don't have a constitutional right to have assisted suicide, it also said that each state is free to write its own laws concerning PAS.[5]

What Do I Need to Know About PAS?

Dealing with death is hard in itself, and dealing responsibly with euthanasia in our volatile times is even more difficult. Responding in an informed, Christian manner demands that we clarify terms even though there is no consensus on how best to define some concepts. These distinctions are taxing, but mastering them is critical as we make wise end-of-life decisions.

Euthanasia

First, we should pin down exactly how we use the word "euthanasia." The word comes from Greek. It combines *eu*, meaning "well," and *thanatos*, meaning "death." Euthanasia is *mercy-killing*, intentionally taking a human person's life for a merciful reason. James Rachels, a philosopher who advocates euthanasia, developed what are now considered the standard criteria for *euthanasia*. According to *Rachels' paradigm*, a case that meets the following five criteria is the "clearest possible case of euthanasia":

1. The person is killed deliberately.
2. The person will die soon anyway.
3. The person is suffering significant pain.
4. The person requests to be killed.

5. The motive of the killing is mercy—to provide as good a death as possible given the situation.[6]

Allowing to Die

Some end-of-life cases don't meet all these criteria. How are we to understand less clear cases?

One issue is those who aren't directly killed. People commonly distinguish between two kinds of euthanasia, *active* and *passive*. Active euthanasia involves acts that positively take a life, while passive euthanasia includes acts that withdraw treatment or aid of some sort. In the former, a physician or other person actually kills the patient, but in the latter, the underlying disease or injury kills him. The difference lies primarily in the physical character of the act, in the means used to reach an end. The distinction centers on the question, What is the biological cause of death? If the cause is physically administered by the doctor (he injects the suffering patient, say, with potassium chloride), then it's a case of active euthanasia. If the physician ceases doing all he can to defeat the disease (say, he decides against chemotherapy), and allows the disease to end the patient's life, then it's passive euthanasia.

To illustrate the difference, consider these two cases. In one situation, a woman was diagnosed with ALS, Lou Gehrig's disease. Gradually, she declined. Without any hope of cure, she asked her doctor for an injection that would stop her heart. When he gave the injection, the patient died.

In another, more common case, an intestinal cancer patient needed an operation. As the surgeon cut open the abdomen, she quickly detected cancerous cells in several internal organs. Knowing that cutting out all the cancer would definitely kill the patient, she simply sewed up the incision. In this case, the surgeon recommended against aggressive chemotherapy, opting instead to concentrate on reducing the patient's pain. Six weeks later, the patient went into a coma and died shortly after. Obviously, it's the cancer that killed the patient, even though the doctor might have added a month or two to his life by prescribing aggressive chemotherapy.

Is the first scenario euthanasia? Obviously, yes. What of the second? Some say yes in that case as well. Those who describe a physician's withholding or withdrawing certain treatments as a kind of euthanasia will use the phrase *passive euthanasia*. In their categories, the first example amounts to *active euthanasia*. The catch, from our point of view, is that using the phrase *passive euthanasia* encourages us to think that *active euthanasia* and *passive euthanasia* describe morally equivalent acts. Rachels defends active euthanasia by appealing to the correctness of passive euthanasia and erasing the distinction between the two. In this way, he tries to transfer the ethical rightness of passive euthanasia to active euthanasia.[7]

Distinguishing active from passive euthanasia is language that encourages the pro-euthanasia movement. So we choose a different way to describe this key distinction. We use *euthanasia* for intending or choosing the death of a person as a means to end suffering. This may be either by directly causing death or by withholding or withdrawing treatment. On the other hand, we use *allowing to die* to refer to acts that choose to avoid useless treatment.[8] Allowing to die intends the well-being of the patient. It never intends death. Rather, a physician purposes to care for her patient's needs as he dies. The physician may know that death will come, but she doesn't choose death as a means to reduced suffering. She may adopt a variety of strategies, but never killing, in her effort to reduce suffering. She may use pain-reducing drugs but will never see death as a "treatment option." In this way, we can bring to the fore the great moral difference between deciding to kill and choosing to care.

By the phrase *allowing to die*, more specifically, we mean an act that meets these conditions:

1. A patient is in the final stages of dying.

2. The person or his legal spokesperson requests or consents to withhold and/or withdraw treatments designed to heal the disease or to attend complications.

3. The doctor withholds and/or withdraws treatments that have no reasonable hope of healing the patient and serve only to prolong the dying process.

4. The physician allows the patient to die of the disease or attending complications, but doesn't intend the patient's death.

5. The physician and the medical staff intend to care for the patient, at least physically (by suppressing pain, for instance), in order that they and others may minister to him emotionally and spiritually as he dies.

In sum, we think it best to distinguish between two different classes of action. The first class is *euthanasia*. Here someone (a doctor, family member, friend, or the patient himself in PAS) intends to kill someone, using death as a treatment option designed to end suffering. The second class is *allowing to die*. Here the physicians and medical staff intend to care for the patient and, as part of that care, to reduce suffering. They will withhold pointless treatments, but never will they choose death.

As alluded to before, three broad positions are possible. First, some support euthanasia. This would mean that they see it as morally right for someone to kill a terminal patient in order to end his suffering. We think this amounts to *disposing of* someone. Second, others reject allowing to die. This would require maximum treatment until the end—keeping the physical body alive at all costs. We think this approach is really *holding on to* someone. (We think both approaches are defective.) Third, one could reject euthanasia but advocate allowing to die. This would imply withholding or withdrawing treatment of a conclusively end-stage disease. But it entails putting a high value on continued care. We call this *letting go*. We defend the view that under the conditions we carefully delineated above, letting go is morally right for Christian physicians, pastors, and families.

Physician-Assisted Suicide

The swirl of controversy today revolves around PAS. Consider Jim, who has worked as a nurse in the oncology ward since graduating from university. Recently he has noticed that his daily jog is too much. He finishes unusually winded and fatigued. At first he attributes it to his age, but as the weeks pass, he is tired even after a good night's sleep. He mentions this to his physician, who arranges for Jim to come in for a checkup. A blood count reveals significant anemia, and his doctor finds a small mass above his right collarbone. A biopsy substantiates Jim's worst fears—it is malignant. Now he is a cancer patient.

Recent advances in treating this form of cancer give Jim hope and courage to go through extensive chemotherapy. But eventually it becomes clear that the treatments can only delay the inevitable. One evening he decides it is time to act. He isn't going to suffer and die as he has seen so many do. He still has some dignity, and he decides his outcome will not rest with someone else. He will be the master of his fate. He will determine when and how he dies. He decides to ask his physician to help him end his own life.

Jim is seeking physician-assisted suicide. PAS occurs when a licensed physician provides information, a prescription, or a device so that a person may take his own life. We believe PAS is a type of voluntary euthanasia. It's the intentional ending of an innocent human life for the purpose of mercy (euthanasia), and the patient chooses that action. (This makes PAS a case of *voluntary* euthanasia—see chapter 6.) But let's be clear: refusing pointless medical treatment isn't PAS. Each competent person who is terminally ill has a right to forgo further treatment, even if that treatment might postpone death for a short time, because, in the end, death will result from the underlying disease.[9] We see this as a case of *allowing to die*.

Jim uses several arguments to defend PAS. One is the rights to freedom and autonomy. Many who imagine themselves in Jim's position ask, "Why shouldn't I take my own life if the quality of my life isn't worth living? It's my life, isn't it?" So suicide is seen as the ultimate expression of personal freedom. In this view, freedom implies complete mastery over one's life. Flowing out of this is the right of self-determination.[10] Many want to control their destinies. These claims fit with our culture's tendency to value individual liberty and absolute self-control (see chapter 1).

Jim also defends a *right* not to suffer. No rational person wants suffering, and we naturally shrink from its grasp. Further, Jim thinks doctors should help patients die because it's the last caring thing a physician can do. In this light, PAS is seen as a final act of compassion. Finally, Jim worries that if he continues the course he's on, he will lose all personal dignity. He resolves that if he's going to die, he will "die with dignity." Again, Jim's notion of dignity is rooted in the values of personal control. The ultimate indignity is losing control, becoming dependent on others, wasting away, and losing all say in what happens. In making these arguments, Jim summarizes why many people today support not only PAS but other forms of euthanasia.

What's Wrong With Euthanasia?

Some people equate euthanasia with murder. This is extreme. Murder is malicious and goes contrary to the desire or intention of the victim.[11] Euthanasia, however, isn't malicious, and it's not necessarily contrary to the patient's desire, assuming the physician has satisfied the requirements of informed consent. Since euthanasia isn't obviously murder, the bankruptcy of euthanasia rests on other grounds.

Moral Problems With Euthanasia

Several lines of thought lead us to reject euthanasia as a morally right act. First, in chapter 2, we said that a moral act has three components: (1) the actor's intention—the goal chosen in performing the act, (2) the act itself—the means we use to achieve the desired ends, and (3) the results—the end we wish to achieve by our act. Think of a telephone solicitor who calls the home of a sincere Christian believer and convinces her to give a substantial contribution to help needy children in the third world. The solicitor is using morally proper means and achieving a good end, but his act is blameworthy if his intentions are selfish—say, if he's motivated by greed because he knows he will pocket one-half of all donations. In measuring any moral act, especially one as significant as ending a human life, we must consider all its facets. Moral decisions are like three-legged milking stools: take away any one leg and the entire line of reasoning falls.

Let's think through these three aspects related to this subject. First, consider intent. Part of the intention behind euthanasia and PAS is, of course, to end suffering, and that's commendable as far as it goes. But another part of the intention is to exert autonomous freedom. Jim's understanding of freedom is inadequate, because it fails to see life as a gift from God. Jim also fails to acknowledge that God has a spiritual reason for creating human life and has a higher purpose for his life. Further, Jim's view of freedom is too broad. In fact, it's so broad it's an illusion. When someone chooses euthanasia, he's using freedom to destroy freedom. By eliminating life he ends the possibility of freedom.[12] Thus Jim's "notion of freedom fosters a radical moral self-centeredness, a supreme act of pride, that denies that our lives however difficult may be instruments in God's hands to shape the lives of those among whom we reside. Much of our freedom resides in the extent to which we give of ourselves freely to others."[13]

Christians don't accept freedom as absolute self-rule, but as relative self-determination. Our freedom is limited both physically and morally. For the Christian, freedom operates morally when it operates within the limits of God's sovereignty. God gave real freedom so we would choose God's wise purpose, not so we could eliminate freedom entirely.

Second, consider the results. A physician's act of taking a dying person's life will end that patient's physical pain. Considering only this, we might conclude that ending a life of suffering is right. This would make sense to Jim, since he believes he has a right "not to suffer."

We admit that no rational person wants to suffer. But eliminating suffering isn't by itself the overriding issue. We believe that the act itself, the means to achieving the end, is important. And in the case of euthanasia, it's unjustified. Humans are never justified in taking a life, in destroying that which bears the image of God, without a divine command to do so. No such general command exists. In fact, a broad ban against killing does exist. Ending a person's life as euthanists want to do, even though it ends suffering, is a morally wrong act. The truism "The ends don't justify the means" applies. We reject euthanasia fundamentally because it's a wrong means to an end.

But further, we should examine other consequences. While it may be hard to see beyond the personal interests of a suffering loved one, there are the long-range societal results to approving of euthanasia. Since pre-Hippocratic times, physicians have given themselves to caring for their patients and healing their diseases. A physician doesn't simply provide a service to a consumer for a fee—like a plumber who fixes pipes for $55 per hour. Doctor and patient enter a covenant relationship (see chapter 1). A patient trusts his doctor to say and do what's good and right, to keep his best interest at heart. Will adding the responsibility to kill suffering patients alter this relationship? What might motivate doctors? "Patients should be confident that the person who was today trying to save their lives wouldn't try to kill them tomorrow," argues physician Robert Orr. "Should this moral absolute be abandoned, the nature of medical care will be irreversibly undermined."[14]

In the Netherlands, physicians have practiced euthanasia for over twenty years because the courts have agreed not to prosecute them. In that country, the fact is that physicians euthanize a large number of patients without their knowledge or consent.[15] This radically changes the doctor's role as healer. It also makes the patient uncertain: he cannot know whether his doctor is coming to save his life or to take it. Few things in life are more sacred than the doctor/patient relationship. Euthanasia cuts at the heart of the trust that makes this covenant workable. By involving the medical profession in bringing an end to an unwanted human life, the ultimate alchemy has occurred: evil is changed into good, and a wrong act is judged to be right because it has been done by a good actor.

Third, we should take another look at intention. What life view, what mentality, we may ask, does the desire for euthanasia reflect? The pro-euthanasia movement "rests upon precisely the same assumptions about human need, health, and the role of medicine that have created our present crisis—the right to, and the necessity of, full control over our fate," argues Daniel Callahan. The pro-euthanasia movement caters to the view that if medicine cannot give us the choice of health, then it should at least give us the choice of death. Thus "the compassion [that euthanasia] seeks is not just in response to pain and suffering. It's more deeply a response to our failure to achieve final control of our destiny."

Ironically, however, our thirst for control turns on us. It's virtually impossible to separate the mentality that seeks euthanasia from one that sees humans as lords over life. This mind-set says, "Life is mine to do with as I choose," rather than "Life is a gift from the Creator." Taking a human life without a divine mandate elevates humans to a level that exceeds the Creator's intention. We try to be as gods, a role for which we aren't well suited. "Legally available active euthanasia would worsen, not help, that crisis."[16]

Another part of the euthanist's intention is to "die with dignity." Dying slowly can be a humiliating experience as the ravages of disease reduce a person to a shadow of his former self. And if our concept of dignity is limited to physical appearance and ability to act, then a slow death isn't death with dignity.

But this understanding is inadequate in light of our true dignity as humans. Our dignity doesn't come from what we can do or how we appear. It comes from who we are, individuals who bear the image of a Creator who loves and values each of us. God revealed the extent of that love and value when he came in human form and paid the penalty on the Cross for our rebellion against his sovereign rule of the universe. Nothing in this life can take that dignity from us—not the ravages of disease, not mental impairment, not the loss of consciousness. If we limit our concept of dignity to what the eye can see, we open the door to killing those whose dignity is hidden on the inside. From a Christian perspective, dying with dignity *includes* taking advantage of all reasonable and available treatments to alleviate suffering. It also includes having confidence that whatever comes, we are always loved and cared for by the God who created and redeemed us.

Practical Problems With Euthanasia

There are also some significant practical shortcomings to choosing death as a means to eliminate suffering, containing costs, or ending "meaningless" life. First, humane, morally acceptable alternatives for dealing with terminal illness are available. If we considered euthanasia a valid treatment option, this could easily overshadow the value of a concept we will describe in the next chapter: "only caring" for the dying. Permitting euthanasia presses important options like hospice care into the background. Euthanasia provides a too-easy means for physicians, families, or society to *dispose of* "problem patients" who have the "indecency" neither to die nor to get well.

Second, examining patients is partly science and partly art. Medical diagnosis is often clear. But at other times it depends on indirect evidence. While usually correct, diagnoses of terminal illness can be wrong. Obviously, euthanasia is an irreversible act. If the diagnosis is incorrect, the patient who is euthanized has no second chance.

Third, to allow euthanasia as a medical treatment option also sets us on the proverbial "slippery slope." At first, death is used to relieve physical suffering. In time, it can be applied to other forms of suffering (emotional—as in a "meaningless life"), and then to the weak, the infirm, and finally to the "nonproductive" members of society. It's not difficult to translate the notion of killing the terminally ill and suffering into killing the nonproductive members of society. When people are no longer active producers and contributors to society, when people begin to think that they take out more than they put in, dying can become a duty. Euthanasia introduces a definite, though subtle pressure that those who have a negative impact on society have had all of life they're allotted, and now, as good citizens, they ought to die. Perhaps the greatest shortcoming of euthanasia is the message it sends to the weak and the sick, the depressed individual who doubts life is worth it: "You're right. Your life isn't worth living. You *should* die." Remember the words of former Colorado governor Lamm:

"You've got a duty to die and get out of the way. Let the other society, our kids, build a reasonable life." To die with that knowledge is the ultimate insult. It's to die in utter hopelessness, a judgment confirmed by one of society's respected representatives, the physician.

Do we really want others to choose whether we live or die? Once physicians can put patients to "sleep" or help them commit suicide, we're on the slippery slope to involuntary death, and no amount of legislation will contain it.[17] The Dutch experience with voluntary euthanasia supports this concern.[18] Might not a physician who has grown weary of treating a patient who's about to die find it more expeditious to reach for his prescription pad and suggest that while there's nothing more he can do to bring healing, he can hasten death? Would this not put the poor, the handicapped, and the elderly at risk? Might it not cause some patients to feel they have a "duty to die," especially if they're becoming a burden financially and emotionally to their family?[19] Might it not erode our interest and research into improving care that reduces pain? And might it not usher an unprepared soul into eternity without God?

Conclusion

Patients and families today are too often confronted with complicated and difficult medical decisions. But another issue looms large when death suddenly becomes a real possibility: If PAS and other forms of euthanasia aren't morally acceptable, then what is? What alternatives are available in those difficult, end-of-life situations?

six

Are There Alternatives to Euthanasia?

The news media and advice-givers flood us with arguments supporting what they claim is the right of individuals to end their lives when they become too meaningless, too painful, or too costly to maintain. Physician-assisted suicide, they say, solves these unpleasant situations. Dr. Kevorkian's reasoning is straightforward: "Let's take the case of the quadriplegic, paralyzed from the neck down. A person could live thirty, forty, fifty years like that. Now, if you wish to do that, that's fine.

But there are some people who do not. It's not a matter of pain. These people must have a recourse to the option I'm offering."[1] Kevorkian's challenge is powerful. But we believe it is inadequate and misleading. It falls short of meeting wise standards of a morally correct act. It runs afoul of God's purpose for human life. It denies our role as stewards of life that bears his image. But if we reject *disposing of* our loved ones, we need help in dealing with the practical issues that arise in making tough decisions at the end of life.

What Is a Morally Acceptable Alternative to Euthanasia?

There are moral and practical alternatives to the evil of euthanasia. We do no service to God and the cause of good by *only* shouting, "Thou shalt not kill!" So the question becomes, What options do we have to keeping people alive beyond their time?

The Rightness of Allowing to Die

We defend the rightness of *letting go*. Under certain circumstances, we believe, withholding useless treatments and allowing the death of a person in the latter stages of the dying process is morally right.[2] In the course of an irreversible disease, we reach a point where treatments no longer improve the patient's condition.[3] At these times, we should simply let go of an earthly life that's ending.

Consider Anna Coughlin, who eight months ago was diagnosed with bowel cancer. The disease has spread to her liver, and soon she will die. Each day she grows progressively drowsier. Tests show her kidneys are failing. Without dialysis, she will die peacefully in about a week. She asks not to be put on dialysis. If I am her physician, do I stand on solid moral ground if I agree to her request? Or am I compelled to try every possible treatment to prolong her life another week until the incurable cancer ends her life?

How does Mrs. Coughlin's request fare in the light of the three components of a moral decision? Both the patient's and the physician's *intentions* are good. The medical staff wants to care for Mrs. Coughlin at the end of her life in a way that allows her to relate to her loved ones as much as possible and to experience as little suffering as possible. The *consequences* are also good. The decision to withhold dialysis will allow her physical anguish to end. If she's permitted to slip away, she dies well. Although treating the kidney failure would give her a few more days of life, her family is by her side, caring and loving her to the very end. It's hard to see how a few days of prolonged dying could make things better than this. And *the act itself*? Surely allowing Mrs. Coughlin's fragile life to slip away follows the first rule of medical ethics: "First, do no harm" (see chapter 1).

The Rightness of "Do Not Resuscitate" Orders

Medical staffs use another method of non-intervention—of withholding treatment—in end-stage terminally ill patients. This is the DNR (Do Not Resuscitate) order. Suppose a patient will die in less than two weeks. After consultation with the patient and/or family, the physician learns that a terminal patient wants no "heroic" intervention in the case of his impending death. The physician writes on the patient's order sheet, "Do not resuscitate." If this patient experiences cardiac arrest, the medical staff makes no effort to do CPR. Is the patient's request morally right? Is the physician morally justified in writing this order? We think so.

Like other cases of withholding treatment, there are times when DNR orders are morally acceptable. There are other times when they aren't. Weighing the morality of these situations is similar to the other cases we have discussed. If a patient is *not* in the end stages of dying from an incurable disease, DNR orders are morally wrong. If a DNR order is written on a chronic leukemia patient who has several years left, for example, failure to attempt CPR is morally indefensible. It omits doing something that has a reasonable expectation of returning the patient to a fulfilling spiritual, emotional, and possibly physical life for some time to come. This act fails to fulfill the duty to beneficence. It is morally unacceptable.

An Objection to *Allowing to Die*

Given the weightiness of end-of-life decisions, some people might find *allowing to die* troubling. Anything less than *hanging on* doesn't feel right. They feel *allowing to die* is too broad and opens the floodgates to all sorts of wrong choices.

Consider this example: Suppose one day, as I walk out of my house, I see little Andrew splashing helplessly in the middle of my neighbors' pool. I realize Andrew will drown unless I act, and it's well within my power to save him. Now I really like Andrew. He's a cute little guy. But I'm wearing a tuxedo and am running late on my way to meet my wife for an important fund-raising dinner. So I choose not to pull him out of the pool, and I don't alert anyone to his predicament. I choose, in other words, to allow Andrew to die.

Is there any difference between Andrew's situation

and Mrs. Coughlin's? Superficially, the cases are similar. Both are examples of inaction or omission. In both instances, I don't *cause* death. I merely *allow* it. In both cases, I could prolong life but choose not to. So the objection to *letting go* goes like this: Allowing Andrew to die is obviously morally wrong, and these two cases are morally equivalent. Therefore, allowing Anna Coughlin to die must be wrong, too. And this means that allowing a terminally ill loved one to die isn't acceptable.

Our answer to this objection requires seeing how these two cases are different in morally relevant ways. First, though, there are obvious similarities in the two examples. Indeed, (1) both cases are acts of omission. In both instances (2) I'm not the physical cause of death, and (3) I could have prolonged life but chose not to. But here's the key: These three factors may be *necessary* for a choice to be an instance of allowing to die, but they're not *sufficient*. The three factors are part of a morally permissible act of allowing to die, but not all cases where these three factors are true automatically qualify as morally permissible acts. The example of Andrew's drowning makes this clear.

In addition to these three qualities, a morally permissible act of allowing to die must meet several other criteria. The main issue is that in Andrew's case, I can perform an act, at minimal cost and with minor negative side effects, that would give Andrew decades of normal life. In Mrs. Coughlin's case, no act I can perform can bring any semblance of extended meaningful life. Because it's well within my power to save Andrew and give him decades of life, my decision not to act to save him can only be a choice that he die. My refusal to save him indicates that I intended he not be rescued. In no sense could I claim I wanted what's best for the boy. I will have killed him. In Mrs. Coughlin's case, however, I can withhold treatment, actively medicate pain, and minister to spiritual and emotional needs. In so doing I clearly intend what's best for her.

We know that all life has an end. Our own deaths and the deaths of loved ones are a reality we all must confront. We must accept that there is a time to die, a time when our best efforts to cure become ineffective, a time when we can no longer hold death at bay. In those cases, *allowing to die* is morally right. To continue actively treating a patient under these circumstances can be as much a violation of that person as withholding useful treatment. In such cases we turn to what one writer called "only caring for the dying."[4] In *allowing to die*, we continue to do what's appropriate for the patient, meeting emotional and spiritual needs and suppressing discomfort. It's the euthanist who wants to cease responding to the patient—to stop curing and then to get rid of the person through death. In *allowing to die*, a person "dies his own death from causes that it is no longer merciful or reasonable to fight by means of possible medical interventions."[5]

How Can We Care for the Dying?

Surely we can do more for our loved one than end her life. We can do what's more difficult: we can stand with her in her hour of death. "If the sting of death is sin," Paul Ramsey says, "the sting of dying is solitude. . . . Desertion is more choking than death, and more feared. The chief problem of the dying is how not to die alone."[6] Turning from futile attempts to cure does *not* mean we're doing "nothing." We turn from what's useless to what's useful—"only caring for the dying."

In our own discomfort with death, we cannot leave our loved one to face her last hour alone. Instead, we must come alongside her during this journey to the end. One of the ways we can do this is found in the revival of an old concept: hospice care.

Hospice Care

Hospices—places where travelers found food, refuge, and spiritual support for their journey—covered the medieval European countryside. The name *hospice* later came to describe places that fulfilled a similar purpose for travelers on their way to the next life. Hospice care became part of modern medicine when Dr. Cicely Saunders opened St. Christopher's hospice in London in 1967. Today about two thousand hospices exist in the United States alone, and roughly one-third are maintained by religious organizations. Hospice care primarily serves the needs of patients in their homes, providing for spiritual, emotional, social, and medical care and support.

What brought the hospice philosophy into mainstream modern medicine? Medical advances made it possible for people to live longer with their diseases. For some, however, that meant taking longer to die. At the same time, medicine's phenomenal technological strides brought an unintentional side effect. As physicians emphasized diagnosis, intervention, and technical support, they put relatively less value on patient care, especially for those who didn't respond well to treatment. Changes in family structure also meant that extended families weren't always available to care for and nurture a loved one whose life was prolonged. So home care for some terminally ill patients wasn't available.

Saunders, trained as a nurse, social worker, and physician, recognized these factors and determined to fill the gap. She envisioned a team approach that would provide care for patients who were too sick to care for themselves at home but not sick enough to enter the hospital for acute care. Families would receive help from visiting hospice workers to provide care at home. When supported home care became unworkable, the dying could move into the homelike atmosphere of an in-patient hospice facility.

One of Saunders' primary concerns was pain control. Symptoms, she realized, strongly influence how the patient views his situation.[7] Pain, she saw, is destructive to the human spirit. It "nails you to your body." This led her to research better means of pain relief. The "Brompton cocktail," which puts drugs like morphine, heroin, and cocaine in a flavored base, given on a regular schedule, became the effective mainstay of symptom relief. There's no dose limit on pain medications. When they're administered only for pain relief, the incidence of addiction is minimal. Drugs that reduce swelling, pressure, cramps, nausea, or depression help patients cope with symptoms.[8]

Hospice workers found that pain is more than a physical response to noxious stimuli. Saunders began to speak of "total pain," a concept that includes psychological, social, spiritual, and physical dimensions. How a patient views his situation profoundly influences how he perceives pain. For example, if the staff doesn't sufficiently appreciate the patient's social needs, his pain is often more intense. When those needs are addressed, however, his physical discomfort is less. Often the most effective medication a hospice worker can offer is human love administered in large doses.

Through an interdisciplinary team of physicians,

nurses, social workers, chaplains, and volunteers, patients are helped "to live until they die." No team member is more important than another, and no one member knows what's best for the patient in every situation. Each patient has different needs, and the team assesses those needs and formulates a plan of care around her individual needs. Ideally, the patient's own physician is part of the team. His presence contributes to continuity of care and reassures the patient that she isn't alone. Nurses not only give direct patient care but also bring the pieces together—the patient's response to care, the family's concerns, and the staff's frustrations—so that the rest of the team can appreciate the big picture. Social workers, chaplains, and volunteers accomplish many important tasks while the medical staff carries out more specialized care.[9]

Family members are involved in patient care. They're taught how to give medication and daily care while the patient is at home. If the family needs respite, a short-term stay can be arranged at an in-patient facility. Should the patient's condition deteriorate to where admission to the in-patient facility is necessary, the family continues as part of the care team. The final stay in the in-patient unit is often one week or less.

A "good death," marked by reasonable comfort and symptom management, is important not only to the patient but to the patient's family. It provides a time for healing estrangements, closing the past, and preparing for the future. When a person dies in hospice care, loved ones often look back and remember a meaningful and satisfying experience. The time of dying was positive, not shrouded in painful sights and morbid experiences. It is good to die in peace.

Hospice is a positive response to the difficult problem of dying. It's a means by which Christians who oppose euthanasia and PAS can, by example, show a better way. Patients who have asked for PAS or euthanasia, when offered hospice care, have frequently changed their minds. It's rare for a hospice patient to request PAS. Patients need not fear dying alone and uncared for, nor do they need to feel helpless and no longer in control. "When someone asks for euthanasia or turns to suicide," Saunders has said, "I believe in almost every case someone, or society as a whole, has failed that person. To suggest that such an act should be legalized is to offer a negative and dangerous answer to problems which should be solved by better means."[10]

The Value of Only Caring for the Dying

Imprinted clearly on the mind of most physicians is the idea that their first duty to their patient is to cure disease and delay death for as long as possible. The fact of death can raise a conflict of roles for the physician. From the beginning, she was taught that Death is the Enemy, one she must fight to the end. She's been well trained to do this, and she tries to stay one step ahead of the Adversary. Continued life means she's still winning. Even in the face of certain defeat, she's prompted to think, "There must be something more I can do—a last-second miracle I can pull off."

Eventually, however, the inevitable comes. When defeat is unavoidable, a physician is often tempted to distance herself from the patient who has, without knowing it, become an ally of the Enemy. She's tempted to relegate the patient to an out-of-the-way room, or she may see the patient on rounds only two or three times a week rather than each day. Out of sight is out of mind. *Terminally* ill comes to mean *hopelessly* ill.

At this point, the physician's role becomes more one of *being* than one of *doing*. It's the role of caring rather than curing. For the physician who has been taught the way of *doing* much better than the art of *being*, this is uncomfortable. It's much easier to write an order for a medication or an intravenous drip of glucose than to sit with the patient, listen to his fears and concerns, and discuss what lies ahead—to assure him that she will be here for him. If physicians are to be more than mere technicians, if they're to be "doctors of the art and science of medicine," they must be care-givers. There comes a time when the best medicine is *being with* rather than *doing for*. This gets to the moral heart of the physician-patient relationship, the covenant they entered into when the person became the patient—a covenant based on fidelity.[11]

Prolonged dying can also produce a sense of helplessness and frustration for family and friends. All people share a sense of discomfort in the presence of death. Brushing elbows with death raises the specter of our own mortality. So family members sometimes stay away from the dying patient. They may try to rationalize their absence with, "If there's nothing I can do, why must I be present?" They sometimes feel more comfortable when not present. But if family members stay away completely, they leave their loved one to die a pitiful death: alone and uncared for. This shouldn't be. This isn't to say that we must be at the bedside twenty-four hours a day. But Christians will want to assure their loved ones of their concern by being present and available.

When Jesus was about to go to his death, he told his followers that he wouldn't leave them without a "Comforter." He would send "another" or one "like himself" who would stand with them, comforting them in life and through death. This was no hollow promise. On the day of Pentecost, the Holy Spirit did come into the world and has been effectively carrying out his work as Comforter, Teacher, and Guide.

We're all called to be "little Holy Spirits," people who come alongside our loved ones not only in life but also in death, to comfort and stay with them to the end. By modeling the presence and care of God to the dying, by coming alongside to love and support them, to read Scripture and pray as well as to provide for physical comfort, we can show a skeptical world that there are good alternatives to euthanasia.

What If the Patient Can't Decide?

A patient's actively choosing an alternative to euthanasia, we argue, is a better way. But in some cases, the patient isn't able to participate in a decision about when to change or to cease medical treatment. Someone else has to make the tough decision. What then?

Advanced Health Care Directives

One distinction is crucial. People typically distinguish between voluntary and involuntary choices. A *voluntary* decision means that a patient participates meaningfully in the decision to end aggressive treatment. *Involuntary*, by contrast, is often used for any case where the patient doesn't participate in the decision.

This definition of *involuntary* is too broad, however. It hides a second important distinction. In some cases, patients can't make treatment decisions because they're permanently incompetent or irreversibly unconscious. A better term for medical decisions made on this patient's behalf is *nonvoluntary*. In other cases, however, patients don't choose their treatment because others take away their decision. The patient *could* make the decision, but someone steps in and pushes the patient aside. This is truly *involuntary*. Due to the principle of informed consent, involuntary decisions are rarely right (see chapter 1). But nonvoluntary decisions are sometimes necessary for incapacitated patients. Our society recognizes several mechanisms for making such choices, and we discuss them below. We believe involuntary decisions—though they may be necessary in some situations, like hospitalizing psychiatric patients—are never right in end-of-life situations.

Whether or not a particular decision is voluntary is very important. According to the principle of informed consent, the patient has a right to determine his future. Heeding a patient's input on any treatment decision, to the degree that it is possible, is one way to love and respect that person. An obvious problem arises, however, when a patient can't make a voluntary choice, and someone else must decide what to do.

In several landmark cases, individuals who hadn't made their wishes known were kept alive to die a lingering death, while others were resuscitated never to regain consciousness. When patients who gave no indication of their desires became incapacitated, the question often ended up in the courts. Long, expensive legal battles finally determined whether to continue or cease treatment. The well-known cases of Karen Ann Quinlan, Nancy Cruzan, and Paul Brophy underscored the need for patients to leave instructions concerning the terminal care they desire. These instructions are *advanced health care directives*.

In an attempt to reduce costly court battles and to allow patients a greater role in determining their final treatments, the federal government enacted the Patient Self-Determination Act of 1990 (PSDA). For the first time, the law focused on the decisions of competent adults to refuse life-sustaining treatment. The law, which applies to all health care institutions receiving Medicare or Medicaid funds, requires that medical institutions provide each adult patient with written information and an explanation about his rights to make decisions concerning medical care, to refuse treatment, or to make advanced directives upon admission. Medical institutions must document any advanced directive a patient makes and include it in the patient's medical record. PSDA has given greater legal weight to several kinds of advanced directives, including the living will and health care durable power of attorney.

Living Wills

Living wills are commonplace. In 1976, California allowed people to put in writing their wish not to have their life extended by artificial means should they become terminally ill. The state protected from criminal charges any physician who followed these written instructions. Today, almost all states have such laws. More recently, institutions are tending to recommend or even require that their patients write a living will. Patients, expecting to have a say in their final medical treatment, are often willing to comply. They want some assurance that hospitals and doctors understand and respect their preferences concerning terminal care.

The concept behind a living will is quite simple. While still physically and mentally able to make decisions about medical treatment during a terminal illness, people prepare a document in which they specify their thoughts about final treatment.

Living wills offer several notable benefits. They allow patients to participate to some extent in decisions about how their final days are spent. The decision to consider signing a living will is also an opportune time for family members to discuss their values and ideas about life and death and how each of them would want to face it when that inevitable time comes. Further, a living will provides the physician with a sense of direction when he must make difficult decisions—when the patient cannot make them.

For all their apparent benefits, however, living wills do have limitations. First, most patients cannot fully understand their implications. On the surface, the documents appear straightforward. The legislative acts that authorize the living will are so written, however, that unless patients modify their own living will, the underlying state laws control how and when the document applies. For example, the Maine statute defines *life-sustaining procedures* as "any medical procedure or intervention that, when administered to a qualified patient, will serve only to prolong the process of dying. 'Life-sustaining treatment' may include artificially administered nutrition and hydration, which is the provision of nutrients and liquids through the use of tubes, intravenous procedures, or similar medical interventions."[12] Patients usually don't know that by signing a one-sentence form, they are in effect adopting the state's definitions of terms. Some would be surprised to learn, for instance, that intravenously administered food and liquid count as *treatment*.

Second, living wills are relatively inflexible. The great majority of states with living will statutes require that physicians follow the instructions in their documents very closely. This offers patients little leeway in tailoring the contents to fit their own wishes for terminal care. Patients will have a difficult time indicating personal desires that lie outside the state's definitions and limitations.

Third, at this time, few states recognize the legitimacy of a living will executed in another state. Although this situation will probably improve, if declarants are hospitalized today in a state other than where they signed their living will, the document often serves only as suggested treatment preference.

Fourth, people can and do change their minds. A living will executed at age forty-five remains legally valid (unless it's revoked or altered), but it may not reflect the person's wishes when he reaches age seventy-five.

Fifth, the presence of living wills in an increasingly litigious society means it's entirely possible that persons with living wills will be undertreated in emergency situations. Of course, had no one invented living wills, we would still have the problem that those without living wills may be overtreated. But just as physicians don't want to be sued for doing too little for those without living wills, they also don't want to be sued for doing too much for those who do have them.

Finally—and most seriously, we believe—a living will can't precisely address a patient's future condition. It's virtually impossible for a person to say in a living will specifically what he wants his physician to do, because this requires knowing well in advance the precise situation he will face at the end of life. This is usually impossible. When people write advanced directives, they generally have certain scenarios in mind. But when terminal situations actually arise, the people may face completely different conditions. By their very nature, then, living wills must be broad and general. They can't take into account the sort of specific issues and realities that always shape the medical decisions people make.

These limitations suggest a cautious approach. Living wills do make known, to some extent, a person's wishes for terminal care should he be unable to provide that information at a later time. In addition, they provide excellent opportunities for families to talk through their values, wishes, and dreams. It is meaningful, even if it feels awkward, to talk through with loved ones your heartfelt desires for living and dying. It could also provide a space to share how profoundly you care about your loved ones. Above all, make the decision to sign a living will with careful consideration.

Because of the limitations of living wills, many people prefer to exercise a health care durable power of attorney or at least to augment their living will by sharing their values and desires with a trusted friend or family member through a limited power of attorney.

Health Care Durable Power of Attorney

A more flexible advanced directive is the *health care durable power of attorney*. All states today have statutes authorizing durable power of attorney. A power of attorney is a document that allows another person to act on someone's behalf. They're *durable* in the sense that the power of attorney remains in effect over time unless it's revoked. In durable health care power of attorney, one person authorizes another to act on her behalf regarding health care decisions should she become incapable of deciding. For example, someone diagnosed with Alzheimer's disease might give her spouse durable power of attorney.

PSDA provides for both a *general* health care power of attorney and a *limited* health care power of attorney.

The general power of attorney assigns to a person who is designated as an *attorney in fact* the power to make *all* health care decisions for the patient who becomes incapacitated. No living will is executed. Should surgery be required or should the patient's physician determine that other treatments are medically advisable, the *attorney in fact* decides what to do—including choosing whether to give or withhold fluid and/or nutrition in terminal care.

A limited power of attorney can bring together the advantages of the living will and the durable power of attorney. The patient indicates in advance, by a living will, his wishes regarding issues like withholding or withdrawing fluid and nutrition in the terminal stages of dying. The power of attorney comes into effect only on the more limited questions not covered by the living will. So, for example, decisions regarding more specific treatments such as surgery or CPR are made by the *attorney in fact*, the person who holds the durable power of attorney. If a patient hasn't made a living will and so hasn't expressed his wishes regarding withdrawing fluid and nutrition, the law understands that the unspecified wishes of the patient are that fluid and nutrition are maintained throughout terminal care.

The advantages of a durable power of attorney over a living will seem obvious. The *attorney in fact* is a trusted advocate who can make current decisions based on the expressed values and wishes of the patient *and* in the light of all the medical facts that were unknown when the living will was signed. Further, instructions given under the close observation of a personal representative are more likely to be followed than those stated in a document executed some time previously and existing as only a piece of paper in the patient's medical record. Of course, the main disadvantage is also obvious. A patient must implicitly trust her health care *attorney in fact* to make decisions in her best interests.

Court-Appointed Proxy

What happens if a patient becomes incompetent to make his or her own decisions and hasn't left an advanced directive? Then a court may appoint a responsible individual to make a particular decision as a substitute decision-maker on the behalf of the incompetent patient.[13] A court-appointed proxy isn't really an advanced directive, because it applies to patients who never really gave any direction to the decision-maker—in fact, the court has to appoint the proxy precisely because the patient didn't give an advanced directive. So obviously, durable power of attorney is better than a court-appointed proxy. Durable power of attorney is easily established prior to the tough decisions. Further, the patient selects the individual, preserving some self-determination for the patient. A court-appointed proxy requires a long and expensive court procedure. Worse yet, the court chooses the proxy, leaving the patient entirely out of the picture.

Once again we face the important question: Who decides? But now the question is at a new level. The legal strategies we've discussed here don't answer the question of who decides who gets to decide. Sometimes, say, when the patient has a competent spouse, the choice of a proxy is obvious. But if a person faces a terminal situation and needs to select an *attorney in fact*, he may still have to work through a process to chose that person. The lawyers can care for the formalities of paper work, but the patient will determine the real content of the legal strategy. As we said in chapter 2, there's no magic way to come to agreements in these cases. The *attorney in fact* must be someone who can put aside self-interest—whether that be a desire to make the decision or to avoid it. He must act in the best interests of the patient. If you must make this sort of choice, get help from wise counselors who can clarify the discussion and work through a decision process with you. A pastor is usually a good choice. And you'll want to ask God for his direction as well.

Conclusion

It's wise to think about who will make end-of-life decisions, either for you or for a loved one. Even with careful preparation, however, the path to the end is most often a difficult one. If we do decide to cease fruitless medical intervention, there's still much to do. Caring at this point in life involves ministering at a spiritual level both to patient and family. At some point you will undoubtedly struggle with the age-old question: Why do we find suffering in a world created by a good God? How can we find hope to survive in times of crisis?

seven

Does Suffering Make Sense?

Margaret was in her early sixties when she came in complaining of a persistent pain in her upper back. She first tried home remedies, but the pain grew worse. Tests showed she had multiple myeloma, a bone marrow cancer that made her anemic, caused severe bone pain, and made her prone to infection. Although I (Peter Emmett) treated her in the usual way, her condition got worse over several months. Office visits were difficult. Any movement, even the jar of her wheelchair over a bump in the sidewalk, was painful. Blood transfusions and narcotic pain relievers helped alleviate some of her symptoms.

Through all this, Margaret never complained. She

smiled often and spoke cheerfully. Her strong faith in God helped her cope with the disease and appreciate what she did have—a loving husband and family, and activities she could still enjoy. She was an avid bird watcher, and she looked forward to telling me about a new or rare bird she had spotted outside her window. When it became clear that death would come soon, I placed her on medications that helped relieve her nausea and pain. She remained at home where she wanted to die. One day a call came from her husband. Margaret's suffering was over; she had entered eternity.

As a young physician, I learned much about pain and suffering from Margaret. Because she found purpose in all of life, she found meaning in her suffering as well. I cannot imagine it ever occurred to her that she should avoid her suffering. Manage it? Yes. Avoid it? No. She was determined that until she died, she would live to the fullest the life God gave her. She did just that even through suffering.

What Do People Say About Suffering?

Pain and suffering are very real, and their ruthless ways repulse us. Suffering is an enemy that perplexes and confuses us—we can make little sense of it. When we watch a loved one suffering a slow and agonizing death, it seems inconsistent with a world ruled by a loving God. We know God can heal and sometimes chooses to do so.[1] But when he doesn't, when patients die by painful inches, euthanasia or PAS can seem like attractive solutions. Death offers the ultimate pain relief. Choosing death becomes an attractive option for grasping control of an apparently uncontrollable situation. Is this our best response to suffering?

The Problem at Two Levels

Usually the word *pain* emphasizes physical experience. Pain is a pressure, a severe discomfort, that we feel somewhere in our bodies. Pain can be an ally. Sometimes it's an alarm system telling us of a problem. A growing pain in a cut finger suggests infection that needs treatment. Crushing chest pain that radiates down an arm warns of heart attack. It urges us to seek immediate help. Without pain to warn us, we'd ignore significant threats to our health. But modest pain, once our friend, can grow into full-blown suffering, our enemy. The word *suffering* includes more than just pain. It's the experience of anguish, of mental, emotional, or spiritual discomfort, that can result from anything we perceive as evil.

When our friend becomes our enemy, when pain becomes suffering, we wonder, *How can a loving God allow this to happen?* This is an ultimate question. It tempts people to deny God's existence. But notice that rejecting God won't make suffering any easier to take. Without God, suffering would still be suffering. Now without God, there would be no intellectual puzzle about why a good God allows evil. Without God, suffering is simply an unpleasant, unexplained reality. An atheist shouldn't view suffering as out of place in the universe as he understands it. But for Christians, suffering raises a theological problem: Why do we suffer when the Bible says we live in a world that is made and ruled by a God who cares about us and who could take our suffering away? How can this be? Where is God?

We experience this difficulty with evil at two levels. One of these is primarily intellectual; it's the classic *problem of evil*. The other is primarily practical or experiential; it's what we call the *problem of suffering*. The first of these is an intellectual puzzle. How do we square up certain Christian beliefs—God exists; God is loving; God is almighty—with the existence of pain and suffering? The problem of evil is a demand for an intellectual explanation. The second problem emerges at the level of everyday life. How can I cope with the frightening cloud that's descending around me, shutting me in, and smothering me? The problem of suffering isn't a demand for an explanation. Rather, it's a desperate cry for resolution.

This distinction is important because the two problems require two different answers. Intellectual answers offered when practical questions are asked seem *hollow*. Someone struggling emotionally will see detached, theoretical explanations as irrelevant, or worse. If I respond to a sufferer who's in the dark night of despair by describing theological theories that explain why God might allow evil, he will probably feel as though I don't understand him. But practical, everyday suggestions shared when intellectual questions are asked seem *shallow*. Someone struggling with doubts needs more than the assurance that God will share his deepest sufferings. She needs solid theological discussion. So we must keep these two problems clearly distinct. Both are important, and both need answers. But the *kind* of answer each needs is different.

How Do We Answer the Intellectual Problem?

Since we believe God is loving and almighty, suffering poses a forceful intellectual dilemma. Though critics of the Christian faith have pressed this point for a long time, eighteenth-century opponents of Christianity framed the question in a specific way, developing what is now called the *problem of evil*. English philosopher David Hume asked,

"Is [God] willing to prevent evil, but not able? then is he impotent. Is he able, but not willing? then is he malevolent. Is he both able and willing? whence then is evil?"[2]

Philosophers have wrestled with this question ever since. Various philosophers try to solve the problem of evil by reducing God's love or power. But these proposals fail because none of them is livable. None holds up under the weight of life's realities.[3] In other words, if we deny the fully biblical view of God, who is at once almighty and loving, we may reduce the *intellectual* tension buried in the question. But this strategy charges a high price. It creates new pressure in everyday life. It reduces the *practical* divine resources available to those who suffer. Those who reject the biblical God have no divine source of strength when walking "through the valley of the shadow of death."

A more adequate answer to the problem of evil depends on the total Christian worldview. Here we learn what Christians have always seen as the purpose of life. Many today—whether rock stars, talk show hosts, or university professors—identify *happiness* as the greatest Good. But for twenty-five centuries, wise thinkers usually defined *happiness* objectively: to be happy was to be good.

The ancients knew something we moderns are now rediscovering: What we *do* follows from what we *are*. *Being good* is a higher good than *feeling good*. According to the Christian worldview, the Good the ancients sought after is found only in God, for God alone embodies the greatest Good. "It's in Christ that we find out who we are and what we are living for" (Ephesians 1:11, *The Message*). We can find ultimate purpose in life in our relationship to God through Christ. If I know who I am and what I'm doing here, in short, if I know the meaning and purpose of my life—to bring glory and honor to my

Creator—I can reasonably expect to find meaning in all my experiences. And this includes suffering.

The alternative perspective emphasizes finding ultimate good in the pleasures of life. If my life has no ultimate meaning beyond my present moment of pleasurable experience, however, how can I make sense of the most difficult aspects of life—namely, my suffering? In this philosophy, suffering becomes an absurd and senseless experience that I despise and seek to avoid at all costs.

This is the philosophy that pervades contemporary American culture. Americans understand happiness as a warm, positive feeling. I'm happy when my team wins or when I enjoy a good meal—anytime I feel pleasure I'm happy. To this we Americans add the implied assumption that humans have an "inalienable right to the pursuit of happiness" and a right to control our surroundings to guarantee this happiness. Happiness in the sense of becoming good through knowing the highest Good is entirely foreign. In today's worldview, suffering has no place. Suffering collides head on with our ideas about the good life. It ought not to be. Suffering is a square in a world of circles.

But maybe there's a better way. Perhaps by giving feeling good a higher place than being good, the contemporary world walks into a blind alley. Maybe our solution lies in an entirely different direction. We need to admit honestly that suffering is disagreeable and painful. But it's helpful to think about what the world would be like—if we might not be worse off—if God miraculously eliminated all struggle from our lives. Perhaps the almighty, all-loving, and all-wise Lord doesn't instantly solve all questions because he has something that's better, in the end, than quick solutions—the resources to cope with suffering in a way that's pleasing to God and better for us.[4]

Our personal experiences of tragedy and suffering are part of the broader story of God's people as told in the Bible. The most basic thing the Bible says about evil and suffering is that sin brings suffering and death. In the Bible's opening pages, we initially find a divinely created world of beauty, harmony, and purpose. We learn that God created our first parents as his image-bearers. This included the assignment of representing God on earth—to care for the earth as God would and to co-labor with God as they lived on earth.

In Genesis 3, however, the tone changes ominously. Eve and Adam surrender to the Tempter, trying to steal power and knowledge that belonged to God alone. Our present world condition amply demonstrates that the human race and all creation feel the results of sin. Gone are the beauty and harmony. In their place are ugliness, disharmony, and suffering.

Thus evil in its various forms invaded God's beautiful world. In short, the Bible's explanation for suffering in a world made and ruled by an all-loving and all-powerful God is the disobedience of the human race. God isn't the cause of our suffering; suffering resulted when humans misused their God-given freedom, the freedom to choose to obey or disobey him. Evil arose from a rebellious act. So we aren't basically good people to whom bad things happen. We're rebels who need to surrender. That's the bad news. In this world, evil and suffering will plague us.

This event of sinful disobedience gives rise to the most basic intellectual answer to sin, what is called the Free Will Defense. Essentially, this defense sees misused creaturely freedom as the cause of all evil and suffering. God gave his highest creatures the gift of freedom because God desired their love. Love, by its nature, cannot be coerced. It's always given freely. Thus God gives the freedom to love and then allows his creatures to exercise that freedom. God can (and does) sometimes override that freedom. But God always allows human persons to choose whether to follow him. When humans choose not to follow God, they sin. Suffering results from sin, and suffering afflicts both the one who sins and others around him. Intellectually, then, this defense says that evil comes as a by-product of human freedom, which God gave intending that we use it to love and serve our divine master.

The biblical story, of course, is that we humans did—and still do—choose sin and now deserve punishment. Jesus came to duel the forces of evil that lie behind our suffering. He displayed his power over evil as he healed diseases, cast out demons, and raised the dead. Yet the Messiah also succumbed to the last enemy, death. But just when it appeared that evil had won, God acted again, unleashing his incomparable resurrection power. On the third day, God demonstrated to all creation his power over sin, death, and suffering by raising the Messiah from the dead. Jesus transformed suffering by using the enemy's power to defeat him. Calvary is like judo, says Peter Kreeft.[5] When evil hurled its greatest force at him, God turned it back, ironically using the power of evil against itself. Evil, caused by God's creatures (including Satan), is doomed, for God will triumph in the end.

How Do I Cope With Suffering Today?

In the meantime, however, we still suffer, our friends still die, and evil still rages about us. The general reality of fallenness still permeates our world. Did Messiah fail? Speaking biblically, the answer is No! At the cross of Christ, God made the checkmate move. At that point, the chess game is in essence over. The power of evil is indeed conquered. But the actors continue to play out their roles, and this means we still have to cope with suffering. How can we do this?

Appreciate that God Knows Our Suffering

The first and most impressive thing is this: God knows all about our suffering. God didn't sit back on a puffy cloud while his image-bearers were tossed to and fro at evil's whim. He entered time/space history and became fully human—he took on human form and flesh, lived like us, and experienced firsthand everything that had gone wrong with his world. In Jesus, we meet the only adequate response to human suffering. Since Jesus is fully divine and one with the Father, God personally experienced the full brunt of evil when Jesus died on the cross. Only the God of the Bible knows our suffering by experience. For this reason, the Bible says that Jesus is our sympathetic "high priest." (A priest identifies with the people and represents them before God.) Jesus earned that right because he lived among us. He knows earthly life, including its sorrow and pain (Hebrews 2:18; 4:15–16). That's why the Old Testament prophesied that the Messiah would be "a man of sorrows . . . familiar with suffering" (Isaiah 53:3).

As a "man of sorrows," Jesus cares about us. In the Incarnation, God experienced our pain firsthand. So he can truly *sympathize* with our misery. He comes alongside and suffers with us. When we feel the anguish of rejection, he understands. He, too, was rejected by those he came to save (Luke 17:25). When our heart is breaking from the betrayal of a close friend, he knows that, too, for he was betrayed (Luke 22:47–48). When we feel abandoned, he understands. On the cross he cried, "My God, my God, why have you forsaken me?" (Matthew 27:46). And most importantly, when we feel the searing heat of loss, he knows. For he stood at the grave of a dear friend, Lazarus, and wept (John 11:35).

I (David Clark) have a very good friend, Loren, whose experience shows just how important it is that someone knows and cares about our suffering. One day as Loren and I were working in our offices, the lights flickered and went out. Thirty seconds later, someone ran in to say there had been a terrible accident. A man named Milt was injured and perhaps dead. Milt was a campus electrician. As Milt fixed a transformer up on a ladder, wind kicked up, and Milt instinctively grabbed the poles of the transformer to steady himself. A huge charge of electricity rushed down one arm, through Milt's chest, and out the other arm. Milt fell to the ground, apparently dead.

When Loren heard, he instantly ran to the site of the accident, several hundred yards away. There he found Jan, Milt's wife, standing to the side, full of terror as paramedics worked feverishly on her husband. When Loren arrived, he ran over and stood right next to Jan. But he said nothing. Instead, he wept.

Milt eventually recovered. But his arms were burned away, leaving only six inches of arm at each shoulder. In addition to the emotional trauma of the original accident and the intense pain of a burn injury, Milt and Jan faced years of frustrating rehabilitation as Milt struggled to master artificial arms.

Several years after the accident, Milt and Jan moved away. At their farewell gathering at church, Jan reflected on the accident. Hundreds of people had expressed their sympathy, scores had helped with meals and rides, several had stayed with Milt for hours when Jan needed time for errands or rest. But the most meaningful response to the ordeal, said Jan, were Loren's tears on that fateful accident day. Loren's complete sharing in Jan's suffering meant more to her than anything else. The remarkable thing is that in just the same way, the God who created one hundred billion trillion stars shares our suffering. He knows and he cares.

Recognize That God Limits Evil

But, we ask, if God knows and cares, why doesn't he do something about suffering? If we're asking God to give us perfect health and lots of wealth in this world—and this is what Western cultures value most—then it will certainly seem that God isn't doing all he should.

But the Bible clearly teaches that God does limit evil. Of course, as the Free Will Defense says, the primary reason for evil is the abuse of creaturely freedom. In the Garden of Eden, God gave Adam and Eve the responsibility to choose rightly. Then early in Israel's history, God again set out two choices: obedience and life or disobedience and death (Deuteronomy 30:15–20). These were neither idle threats nor bribes. They're part of God's moral management of the world. Doing right—generally and in the long run—results in the well-being of those who do the right, and doing wrong—in the long run—results in punishment for the wrongdoer. In the short term, of course, this may not always happen. Sometimes evil prospers for a time. But in the long run, we generally reap what we sow, and we reap in proportion to our sowing (Psalm 34:11–22).

If it seems that evil is out of hand, however, remember that God's mercy restrains evil. To an ancient king who raged against God, God said, " 'I will put my hook in your nose' " (Isaiah 37:29). This metaphor pictures the evil king as a large, angry bull who's controlled and limited by a slight tweak of his tender nose. If God allowed human evil full sway, we would have destroyed the race by now.

Of course, we might still insist that God limit evil more aggressively. Why doesn't God just eradicate all evil and its consequences? A biblical character asked this same question. He was an honored and righteous man, the cousin of Jesus Christ. His name was John the Baptist. Despite playing a crucial role in announcing the Messiah's coming to the world, John was unjustly imprisoned for preaching against King Herod's sins. As he lay languishing in prison, he began to doubt. He sent word to Jesus: "Are you the Messiah?" (Matthew 11:3). We can certainly understand John's questioning. Wasn't Jesus the savior of Israel? Wasn't Jesus here to overcome evil? "So why," John probably asked himself, "am I still rotting in this prison?" Were I in John's shoes, I'd be looking for an angelic SWAT team to get me out! *Where are you, God?*

The answer Jesus gives to John's emissaries is interesting: " 'Go back and report to John what you hear and see: The blind receive sight, the lame walk, those who have leprosy are cured, the deaf hear, the dead are raised, and the good news is preached to the poor' " (Matthew 11:4–6). Jesus is telling John that on the big scale, much is being done. God is reversing evil at many levels. And most importantly, a message of spiritual salvation— "Good News"—is being preached. John might think that releasing jailed prophets should be part of Jesus' list. But John learned this important truth: If God isn't dissolving my problem right now in the way I find most appealing, I shouldn't conclude that God is doing nothing. Indeed, God is very active. And in the end he will reverse all wrong.

In a sense, John was asking not too much, but too little. He wanted Jesus to be focused exclusively on his own imprisonment when Jesus was working on a bigger plan. As John was wondering whether his life in prison proved that God didn't care, Jesus was moving toward a date with a Roman cross by which he would conquer suffering forever. The solution God has in mind is heaven. More than anything else, heaven is God's presence. A deep love relationship with God marks the citizens of heaven. While John wondered whether Jesus was doing anything, Jesus was doing the greatest thing: making a way so that all human persons could have an eternal love relationship with their Creator.

Embrace God's Gift of Hope

A righteous man of ancient times learned a lesson not unlike John's. The Bible says that Job, a man with vast wealth and a large family, lost everything but his life. He was left with literally nothing—except God. God's answer to Job didn't come as a carefully reasoned explanation. It seems Job went to his grave not knowing why he had suffered. God's answer to Job was a Person: "Job, *I* am your answer." Part of what we learn from Job is that we may not know why we suffer. An exhaustive search for an intellectual explanation for specific experiences of suffering can come up dry.[6] We may know why evil *in general* occurs—say, because humans misuse God's gift of freedom—without knowing why *this particular evil* occurs. We also learn, however, that the answer we need to suffering may not be primarily intellectual. We need, not explanation, but relationship. That's the answer God gave Job, and it's appropriate to us as well. God offers himself.

The reality of God's presence is the most important theme the Bible offers to those in suffering. Christian hope isn't "hope so" hope. That so-called hope lacks confidence. It's a long shot, a throw of the dice, a desperate optimism without any basis in fact. Hope in the Bible is the confident expectation that God will fulfill his promises. It grows out of faith and results in love. (These three virtues appear together in 1 Corinthians 13:13; 1 Thessalonians 1:3; Galatians 5:5–6; Hebrews. 6:10–12; and 1 Peter. 1:21–22.) For those who had experienced Christ's work, the best is still to come. Hope gives believers a sense of assurance, in the face of suffering and death, that life is meaningful after all. Those who believe that good will triumph in the end can cope with the deepest suffering. Those who don't give up in short order.

Christian teacher R. C. Sproul tells a story that makes this point perfectly. He and his wife had just arrived home from a vacation, full of that great "getting home" feeling. As they unloaded suitcases in the garage, the kitchen door opened and their married daughter, Sherrie, blurted out, "Oh, Daddy! My baby is dead!" The mood changed in a flash. The Sprouls dropped the suitcases and moved into the house to share the grief.

Sherrie, about to give birth to her first child, had just come home from a checkup. The obstetrician could not find a heartbeat. As gently as possible, he had broken the bad news: The baby inside her was dead. For medical reasons, the doctor said, Sherrie would have to deliver her dead child. All the agony of labor and childbirth lay ahead. There was no other way. The next day, the family went to the hospital. The physician induced labor, and Sherrie experienced all the trauma of childbirth compounded by the heavy knowledge that the baby was already dead.[7]

Reflecting on this incident, Sproul compared a normal childbirth with Sherrie's experience. In both cases, the pain is excruciating. But in the one case, the woman is thrilled, and the pain is ancient history the instant that new life is laid in her arms. In the other case, the woman fears, resents, and detests the pain, knowing that in the end she will cuddle a dead child for a few brief moments and then bury her firstborn. The physical pain is the same. The emotional response couldn't be more different. What makes all the difference? Hope.

Hope makes all the difference. We don't have all the answers. But we have a God who's bigger than our suffering—even suffering at the end of life. And we can trust him in the end.

Conclusion

We believe these truths are like water on parched lips. But they don't make suffering easy. The most basic thing to say about pain is that it's painful, and that as much as we would like to avoid suffering, it's inevitable. Various techniques for managing pain don't eliminate pain; at best they reduce it. In the same way, death is an inevitable reality. We may seek to delay death, but we never evade it. Thus we must face head on the matter of Christian dying. What's the Christian approach to death? How can families let their loved ones go? How can Christians die well?

eight

How Can Christians Die Well?

Patty Lundborg died of cancer last Friday. Patty was the mother of two beautiful young girls. Her husband, in his mid-thirties, serves on staff at a large, thriving church. They were once a model family. Now they're a model family without a wife and mother. Their story raises unanswerable questions at every turn. What is true for the Lundborgs is true for all the terminally ill: Living with a loved one under the thunderclouds of inevitable death forces us to find strategies for coping. How can we prepare for death?

How Can I Face the Reality of Death?

Thinking of death even in abstract terms is unpleasant. We all say, "I will die someday, of course—everyone does, after all." Still, this is quite different from "This cancer will kill me in three months." If honestly coming to grips with death in the abstract is understandably difficult, thinking about death—my own or a loved one's—in a specific and pointed way is far past upsetting. A moment's reflection on this obvious fact helps us understand why patients and their families and friends often deny bad news. The defense mechanism of denial helps us survive the initial shock of hearing that death will come sooner than we thought.

The symptoms of denial vary. Based on her experience as an oncologist, Ruth Kopp identifies several ways people express denial. One is partial deafness. When a physician tells her patients about their situation, they absorb only part of the information. Significant details about the severity of the disease, the treatment plan, or the possible side effects of the treatment are lost. Patients often cannot describe their condition accurately. For example, Kopp cites patients who suffer from incurable high blood pressure. Since the medication they need will reduce the symptoms but not cure the disease, she tells her patients that they must take the pills indefinitely—and must continue on the medication even if they feel quite well. Yet many patients later ask when they can stop taking the medication or ask about how long it will take to get cured.

Another indication of denial is blindness to symptoms. The fear of a negative report leads some people to ignore trouble signs. They interpret serious symptoms as minor irritants. Sometimes individuals pass off classic symptoms of heart attack, for example, as heartburn, and then take heavy doses of antacids. Even doctors do this!

Denial can also take the form of a search for a better prognosis. Some who receive a bad report go immediately to other doctors or clinics, hoping to find someone who offers a more optimistic report. They may also look to unconventional medicine—untried therapies, New Age healing, or alternative medicines—in hopes of a cure. In Christian circles, some desperate souls searching for a better prognosis will look to so-called faith healers for a miracle cure.

Of course, a second opinion is surely right when a diagnosis is very pessimistic or when a recommended treatment plan includes extraordinary and invasive action. On the other hand, if two or three physicians agree on a serious or terminal diagnosis, looking for "better" medical opinions is often simply denial.[1]

Denial is also displayed in patients' unwillingness to describe their condition out loud. When asked about their situation, they can tell an entirely different story than the medical staff told them. They may actually believe their own version of their case. In one instance, a man who was actually quite near death assumed that one slightly better day was the sign of things to come. He and his wife proclaimed to their friends that he was getting better and going home perhaps in a few days.

Responding to denial takes skill. First, of course, we may find denial in ourselves—whether about our own illness or that of a loved one. Whenever a physician tells someone he's terminally ill, the temptation to deny is real. In fact, almost every patient goes through at least a short period of denial. Sometimes whole families succumb to this temptation with a kind of unspoken agreement where each denies *to the other family members* the full severity of the patient's condition. In this way, an entire family plays a game, each one maintaining a fictional world of optimism on the assumption that others are ignorant of the truth and should be shielded from it. So the patient "protects" his wife; the wife "protects" her husband; both "protect" the children; everyone "protects" the church.

Denial may seem the easy route, because it sidesteps painful thoughts of separation. Yet it's really destructive. At its root, denial is dishonest. Those involved don't face reality. And what they miss is everything valuable that can happen in the last months and weeks of a terminal illness. People can say what they have long wanted to say to those they love. They can express their loves, their fears, their sorrows, and their good-byes. As long as people play the denial game, however, these tender words and the relational closeness or healing they bring remain impossible. "Saying good-bye" requires that the family admit they will soon part. Those who stay clouded in denial to avoid the pain of parting actually eliminate the possibility of healing their pain through real sharing with the ones they love.

Wise families admit their own vulnerability in these periods of enormous stress and courageously ask others for the help they need. Just as there's no shame in requesting that a surgeon operate on the ravages caused by cancer, so there's no disgrace in calling on the pastor to aid with tattered emotions.

We should begin overcoming our denial of death long before terminal illness or catastrophic injury strike. A wise Christian wrote, "I am convinced God wants believers to 'die slowly.' Believers are not to cling to the trappings of this life till the very end. Rather we should slowly lose our grip on this world as our affections are gradually transferred to the next. This must start early in our Christian lives, as we learn to accept our own mortality."[2] Death is real. It will occur. Preparation for holy dying cannot begin until we finally accept this reality.

How Can I Avoid the Longing for Explanation?

When a diagnosis of terminal illness or injury confronts us, most of us immediately ask, "Why me?" This questioning is common in all cases of difficult news. In chapter 7, we discussed how people approach experiences of suffering at two levels. One level is intellectual, the problem of evil, which looks for explanations for evil's existence in a world created by a good God. The other level is practical, the problem of suffering, which searches for coping strategies to survive traumatic times.

In discussing biblical themes, we noted that Scripture at least partially answers the great "Why?" at the level of the cosmos and the human race. But it's one thing to explain evil in general. It's quite another to say why *this specific case* of suffering has happened. As much as we want resolution, we're often unable to discern clear and precise answers to the great "Why?" *at a personal and individual level*.

The urge to explain can be so strong that we even find ways to explain the unexplainable. We identify UFOs, for example, by labeling them *unidentified*, and that oddly satisfies our desire for identification. Once we label them as unknown things, we know what they are! Explaining accomplishes at least two good goals. For one thing, it satisfies an itch, an intellectual curiosity God himself put in us. For another, it helps us get control. If I hear a bad sound in my car, I take it to my mechanic. He looks at the car and explains the problem. With that information, I'm now in control. I can choose to live with it, have the mechanic fix it, or get rid of the car. Once I know the cause, I feel more in control.

Our natural human desire for explanation is helpful. And talking things through with family and loved ones can be positive. But a too-strong desire for explanation of *this particular suffering* becomes destructive. When it comes to great imponderables like suffering, the explanation/control dynamic can get us into trouble in several ways. We can look for explanations of suffering when there are none available. Of course, we can get explanations of a sort from medicine: "John has liver cancer because the cancer cells spread to the liver from the lungs." But these explanations aren't all that helpful. When suffering is great, they seem hollow. They amount to explaining in a *shallow* sense. With a more minor problem, like an infected cut, a shallow explanation that refers to bacteria and their habits would satisfy. In cases of major catastrophe, however, we look for something *more*, something *deeper*. We want answers to the big "Why?" And this is something we can't always know.

It may seem unspiritual or unbiblical or untheological to say, "We don't know why Matthew has pancreatic cancer, and we shouldn't spend too much energy trying to find out." The desire for explanation is so deeply ingrained that most of us fall into it immediately when we hear of tragedy. Recall the Bible story about Job, a man who suffered far more than most of us ever will. His "comforters"—an odd thing to call them—immediately sought to explain his suffering by saying things like, "Job, you've sinned before God. God is punishing you. Confess your sin." Note that their strategy is geared to explaining and controlling the problem. If they're right and Job accepts their prescription, he can end—that is, control—the suffering. But the story doesn't vindicate their approach. In the end, God doesn't offer explanations. He reveals himself.

Note, too, the story of Jesus and the blind man (John 9:1–5). Jesus refuses to be part of explanations that assess blame. He responds to the man's suffering, of course, and uses the occasion to teach about the light of the world. But he also insists that the disciples' speculations about the causes of the man's blindness are fruitless.

The Bible offers many interpretations of suffering. "Evil brings patience." "It's the result of sin." "It brings glory to God." We make a mistake, however, if we turn biblical *themes* too quickly into *theories*, that is, if an idea relevant to some cases evolves into a hypothesis that we assume will explain all suffering. This can happen when people turn something they learned in their own experience of pain into a comprehensive theory for assessing other peoples' experiences of suffering.

In the short run, we shouldn't worry too much about what everything means. God knows, but we don't. If a Christian's experience of illness leads to some spectacular benefits—unbelieving family members receive Christ, new candidates are challenged to missionary service, spiritual maturity is nurtured in those who love him—all that is fine. If we're never able to notice even one positive benefit coming from someone's pain, however, this is fine, too. Each life is valuable to God. It is its own justification. It needs no external results or benefits to justify it. If these come, fine. If they don't—or, more likely, if our finite eyes cannot see any—that must be fine, too.

Why does God choose not to explain all of these things to us? It's not likely that knowing the reasons would help. Consider the case of Jeremiah. While writing Lamentations, he expresses deep sorrow over the ruin of Jerusalem. Jeremiah, in this case, knows the reason: the Jews had faithlessly abandoned their covenant with

God. Knowing this, however, didn't help Jeremiah in the least. He still felt the same sense of despair.[3] We're tempted to believe that answers to the big "Why?" will take away the pain, but often they don't.

What Is the Role of Expectations?

James Dobson points out that some people die quite willingly. Martyrs choose to die rather than to give up their faith. Soldiers jump on grenades rather than to allow their comrades to be hurt. These individuals suffer the greatest harm, yet they don't struggle with the meaninglessness of their deaths. Their deaths have meaning because of a broader set of beliefs into which their experiences fit. Embedded in those sets of beliefs are expectations of what *should* happen to me, what my life *ought* to be like.[4]

This was the worst part of Job's problem. He responded with considerable faith to the enormous tragedies that initially befell him. At the end of the first round of testing, Job simply praised God, and "in all this, Job didn't sin by charging God with wrongdoing" (Job 1:22). Later, however, things grew harder. The intensity of Job's anguish increased because his so-called "comforters" kept harping on their theme: Good people shouldn't suffer. Someone who follows God ought to prosper. The contrast between what Job's companions thought should happen and what really did happen made the suffering worse.

In the course of the story, God seemed far away. This makes Job's suffering worse. In his last speech, after declaring his own innocence, Job cries, "Oh, that I had someone to hear me!" (Job 31:35). If only God would speak. In the end, God answers Job, but the answer isn't at all what anyone expected. "God doesn't explain. He explodes. He asks Job who he thinks he is anyway. He says that to try to explain the kind of things Job wants explained would be like trying to explain Einstein to a little-neck clam. . . . God doesn't reveal his grand design. He reveals himself."[5]

Two fascinating facts emerge at the end of Job's story. The first is that the Lord's response apparently satisfies Job. "My ears had heard of you but now my eyes have seen you. Therefore I despise myself and repent in dust and ashes" (Job 42:5–6). Job doesn't seem to need a full explanation. His faith is such that when God reveals his own presence to Job, it's enough.

The second fact supports this. Job's response is clear *before* the epilogue of the book in which God restores to Job the things he lost. Given what Job has already said, however, we get the sense that this restoration wasn't all-important to Job. He had God; that's really what he needed. Job apparently understood that we don't need God to give us wealth, health, comfort, and pleasure; we need God to give us himself. As long as we believe that absence of pain and suffering is what we have a right to expect from God, we will face disappointment.

One person who suffered personal tragedy made an analogy between living life and taking a trip. Imagine that we plan a trip to Italy. We get excited about the prospects—the catacombs, Michelangelo's David, St. Peter's Basilica, and everything else. We study about Italy and learn a few Italian phrases. We take off and soon arrive, only to find we're in the wrong place. We're in Holland, and we must stay. What to do? We could spend a good deal of time worrying about not being in Italy—hating Holland because it's not Italy or resenting God for giving us an aircrew with inferior navigational skills. Or we could enjoy Holland. It's not Italy, and it's less flashy, but it's a good place. We can enjoy Holland as long as we lay aside any expectations that we really should be in Italy.[6]

Similar logic applies when we face untimely death. If a virile young man lives for seventy years, loves and serves God, raises a family, and all the rest—that's Italy. It would be a good life. If he lives for twenty-five years, loves and serves God, but does *not* raise a family and all the rest—that's Holland. It differs from Italy, but it's still good. Whatever happens, his life can be a good one. His family and church can love him. God will love him. And that would be a good life, also.

How Can I Transform My Perspective?

Sooner or later, however, explanations and understandings must emerge. Critical to our understanding of death is a transformed, heavenly point of view. One of the most remarkable of Paul's statements is this:

> Therefore we do not lose heart. Though outwardly we are wasting away, yet inwardly we are being renewed day by day. For our light and momentary troubles are achieving for us an eternal glory that far outweighs them all. So we fix our eyes not on what is seen, but on what is unseen. For what is seen is temporary, but what is unseen is eternal. (2 Corinthians 4:16–18)

Many Christians fear the "so-heavenly-minded-no-earthly-good" syndrome, so they don't relate well to Paul's affirmation at first. They're afraid to count the next life as more significant than this. We believe, however, that life with God in heaven truly is the better life.

It's the life we were created to enjoy. Indeed, the experience with God we now enjoy is heaven reaching back into this world.[7] For Christians to see this life through the lens of eternity isn't pie-in-the-sky escapism. It's to be in touch with highest Reality, God himself.

Of course, sometimes it doesn't feel this way, especially when we face terminal illness or severe accident and endure the pressure of intense physical pain. We don't mean that this life is without meaning. It's precisely because the next life is so real that our lives now truly matter. The connection between this life and the next means that a clear sense of God's kingdom is indispensable to this life. Because becoming good—instead of just feeling good—is part of our preparation for the next life, what happens to us here and our reaction to it are critically important. So Paul encourages us to "fix our eyes" on what's yet to come.

Author Max Lucado imagines a story where three children lose an older friend. That friend, Josh, wrote them a letter to help them understand death. Josh's wife, Melva, reads, and soon she comes to this passage:

> Many think death is when you go to sleep. They are wrong. Death is when you finally wake up. Death is when you see what God has seen all along.
>
> I want you to do something for me. I want you to think about [newborn] babies. Imagine what has happened to them. They have just left one place and entered another. Just a few hours ago, each one of them was in a mommy's tummy. They were safe. They were warm. They had all they could eat. All they had to do was sleep.
>
> Suddenly they were pushed into a strange world that they had never seen before.
>
> Imagine you could speak to one of these infants

before he was born. What if you told him what was about to happen? What if you said, "In just a few minutes you are going to leave this tummy. Your time in here is about up. Before you know it, you will be in a room full of people and lights and noises and smells . . ."

"I don't want to go," the baby might say. "I like it here. Besides I don't know what a 'people' is."

"Oh, you don't need to worry. It's not bad out there," you'd tell the infant. "I mean, you have to go to school and take baths."

"What's a school and a bath? None of that sounds good to me. I like it right here."

"But it's dark in there. It's crowded and cramped. Don't worry. You'll be glad you came out."

"Thanks, but no thanks. I'm happy where I am. I want to just stay right here."

Later, Melva finishes the letter:

> Eric, Landon, and Shannon, it's time for me to leave. It's my turn to go and be with God in heaven. I don't want you to be afraid. I'm not. It's my time. I accept that. It's okay to be sad, but don't be angry; don't be scared. God knows what He's doing.[8]

Perspective makes all the difference.

The difference between an earthly perspective and a heavenly one becomes clear when we contrast our culture's usual view with the attitude common in the Middle Ages. To moderns, the life that counts is this one; preparing for another world isn't part of our agenda. Thus when death comes, we hope only to make it as painless and uncomplicated as possible. We hope we won't suffer, and we hope we won't burden others. Our most common wish is "I want to die in my sleep." By contrast, most medievals sought a slower death that allowed them to think through the implications of their lives and to prepare for death. To moderns, with a worldview ruled by the desire to stay in control and to feel comfortable, this seems unfathomable. But to Christians influenced more by Scripture than by contemporary culture, this should make sense.[9]

How Can I Nurture Christian Hope?

A heavenly perspective centers on hope. Although meaning sometimes emerges from terminal illness and death, at other times it doesn't. One thing, however, is constant: how Christians view the future from the perspective of hope. Christian hope radically alters our view of death. The Bible says we are not to grieve as those who have no hope (1 Thessalonians 4:13). This texts implies that *Christians will grieve*. Death is a horrible power unleashed on the world. Paul describes death as "reigning" over the human race (Romans 5:12–21). Death isn't a "natural transition." To say that "death is just a natural part of life" denies the horror of death.

But the Bible also says that *Christians will grieve differently*. This is because the Bible balances an honest view of the tragedy of death with the dramatic truth that Christ, in his resurrection, has already overwhelmed death: "God raised [Jesus] from the dead, freeing him from the agony of death, because it was impossible for death to keep its hold on him" (Acts 2:24). For this reason, Paul mocks death in these stunning words:

Death has been swallowed up in victory.
Where, O death, is your victory?
Where, O death, is your sting?
The sting of death is sin, and the power of sin

is the law. But thanks be to God! He gives us the victory through our Lord Jesus Christ. (1 Corinthians 15:54–57)[10]

We stand between the initial event that guarantees victory over death and the final event when that victory is completely fulfilled. The "death of death" is already real through Christ's resurrection, but it's not yet complete—not until we, too, participate in resurrection. So we rest in a position of Christian hope. The unconditional surrender of death is still future, but it's assured. In the meantime, hope is difficult, but real. It holds tenaciously to God's promise to bring something new out of despair and fear. This "faith may be difficult to attain. Yet precisely because it faces all the powers of defeat squarely, it is difficult to shake."[11]

How Can I Value Holy Dying?

For those who nurture the perspective of Christian hope, death is an entirely different experience. Death cannot ultimately threaten believers. So the Bible remarkably portrays a holy dying as something that can honor God. The psalmist says, "Precious in the sight of the LORD is the death of his saints" (Psalms 116:15). Christians may appropriately submit to the Lord in their dying. This is especially true if the person's life goals are achieved, and no new plans are emerging. There's a certain completeness to a life lived for God. This is especially apparent in the life of an older believer whose task on earth is apparently finished.

On the other hand, it's harder when a young person is struck down in the "prime of life." Why would God allow a young medical student, dedicated to a life of missionary service, to be struck down by cancer just as he's ready to embark on a life of sacrificial service? Such questions haunt us, especially when they involve terminal illness in children. Yet all we have said still holds. Often these imponderable questions are, from a human perspective, largely unanswerable. Obsession with the great "Why?" only begets frustration. Faith in an all-knowing God admits that God knows the whys and wherefores even when we don't.

We cannot, in the vastness of our ignorance, say with certainty that a particular life wasn't complete. Only an expectation that each person must live to a certain age—seventy, eighty, or ninety—in order to live a full life could lead us to say that a life of ten years or ten weeks is incomplete. The question becomes, On what grounds do we rest our expectation that only seventy-, eighty-, or ninety-year-old lives are complete? Indeed, if we have faith in God's providence over individual lives, we must admit that a shorter life can honor him even as a longer one.

To some, this will seem a cop-out. We admit that Christians often give up the search for understanding too quickly. But there's a big difference between admitting that we are stumped by a mystery after we have struggled with tough questions, and jumping directly to mystery the moment questions are asked. Simplicity before complexity differs from simplicity after. We see no connection between the foolish simplicity of the school-boy and the cautious wisdom of a veteran pastor. If the schoolboy says that life is simple, we shake our heads. If the pastor says so, we will sit and wait. He will tell us—and we will listen—that in the end, we must trust our Creator, who alone gives life the meaning we long for.

Some believe that suffering is sufficient cause to sacrifice a human life through euthanasia. We must say that we're as repulsed by human suffering as anyone. We don't desire it, for ourselves or others, even though we know it sometimes brings good results. We know that joy and the good life don't come simply by avoiding suffering at all costs. Joy emerges when we learn to live with pain and find meaning in it. If and when suffering comes to us, we're confident that God will accompany us in it. God will be at work in it, not necessarily to remove it, but to turn it toward good for those who love him. We must use appropriate medications at our disposal to alleviate and manage suffering. We must also learn the life of faith by which God enables us to overcome the fear of death.

Conclusion

The answers of mature Christians to the painful moral dilemmas at the end of life will differ markedly from others' responses. Like everyone, Christians today must deal with the institution of medicine—its assumptions, protocol, and physically oriented methods. Yet we also infuse our use of medicine with a biblical perspective. It's a viewpoint that refuses to see individual health and human control as the ultimate source of meaning. It insists instead on humble faith in God as the center of all that's good. For believers who faithfully adopt this stance, the struggles at the end of life become yet another venue in which to glorify the Creator, for from him alone comes all that is good.

nine

How Can We Go Home?

This book raises the most difficult questions humans ever face: the meaning of existence and life's core values, the bewildering complexity of ethics and controversial moral decisions, the joy of living and pain of dying. These are truly tangled and imponderable questions.

Proponents of euthanasia and PAS want to reduce what they see as meaningless suffering. In itself, this is surely a noble goal. Since we reject their response to suffering, however, what can we say to the reality of human anguish? Can it justify an intervention that sacrifices a human life?

Suffering is surely an unwelcome invader into a

world created good by God. At first blush, pain does seem inconsistent with the ways of a loving and almighty God who could, if he wanted, wipe out evil. But a review of what God has said and done about our suffering shows us otherwise. Suffering remains part of our world, but we're wrong if we conclude that an uncaring God has failed to act against evil. The Bible teaches us that God has personally experienced the totality of evil, including suffering at its worst, and has defeated it thoroughly in Christ. While he allows suffering to remain in our world, it will not overwhelm God. Evil is on a long tether, but that tether is tightly tied.

Since God permits suffering, how are believers to respond to it? The Christian worldview sees everything in this world from God's eternal perspective. Though evil and suffering are part of that world, they don't have the last say. When our own and others' suffering overwhelms us, we cry out, "Does God really care?" Then he invites us to look back to the empty cross where our faith was born. At the moment when it appeared that God was absent, when he didn't intervene but allowed his own Son to suffer and die, he wasn't absent. God was there. It was at the one point where none seemed prepared to find him—in the suffering and dying Christ. The presence of God was missed, overlooked, ignored, because God chose to be present where none expected to find him—in the suffering, shame, humility, powerlessness, and folly of the cross of Jesus Christ.[1] At Easter, God overturned the world's verdict that God is weaker than our suffering and death. Because he has experienced our suffering and defeated it, we know that even in the worst situations God is working for our good.

With the apostle Paul, we can realize that while we *reside* in a fallen world beset by suffering, we *live* on the

Easter side of Calvary, and we live *in* the Christ of Easter. Suffering is very real, but it doesn't destroy us. It confuses us, but it doesn't drive us to despair. Suffering can be excruciating, but we don't experience it alone. It may bring us to our knees, but it doesn't destroy our faith (see 2 Corinthians 4:8–9). In Christ we can know a peaceful confidence that when our times are in God's hands, we're safe. This is no fairy tale, no fantasy. It has been pounded out on the anvil of human experience by many of God's saints, both great and small.

Preparing to Meet Our Maker

But one final issue remains. What if you or your loved one cannot say with confidence, "I'm ready to 'meet my Maker' "? What if you feel unsure about the future? How could you come to know that you or your loved one is safe in God's hands?

Getting ready to meet our Creator, reaching peace with God, is the most important thing we humans can do. At its core, being in God's good graces means to be in a relationship of trust and faithfulness with God. It's a covenant we described earlier—a permanent, giving relationship of faithfulness and caring (see chapter 1). To be at peace with God is to be in covenant. To be in covenant means to have our sins forgiven, to be fully accepted, and to experience the Lord's love forever.

But how can you or a loved one enter a covenant relationship with God?

Faith is the act of entrusting your life into God's care based on Christ's death on the cross. Faith requires ceasing to try to make it into heaven and God's good graces by human effort. It means turning away from all self-centered sin. If you turn from self and sin and call out to God, he has promised to hear you and forgive you. God doesn't want your efforts, your ideas, your accomplishments, your wealth, your reputation, or anything else. He just wants you. To be at peace with God is to say "I do" to him, to trust him, to serve him, and to love him for the rest of your life on earth and for eternity. And it means to receive as a free gift his mercy and forgiveness.

If you're a patient who will soon pass into eternity, you can trust God now and be at peace. That's all God wants. And if you're a family member who's thinking about eternity because of your loved one's experience, you, too, can trust in God and serve him for the rest of your days. This is the purpose of your life, and you will experience the richness of life that God intends only if you enter this new relationship with God.

The reestablishment of relationship with God is called reconciliation. Reconciliation is a healing of broken relationship. Each human sins, and this sin breaks relationship with God. If you try to live life your own way, you will have baggage and burdens. But God invites you to give these up, to let go, and to trust in him. It's as simple as saying to God aloud or in your heart, "I've done wrong. I have sinned, and I receive the gift of Christ's death on my behalf. I trust you, God, to care for me now and in eternity." This is life's most important decision. We invite you to do this now.

If you are a Christian watching a loved one die, this relationship with God can't be forced. It is accepted freely. But with permission, you may speak about these things with your loved one openly, the way you have come alongside your loved one in other crucial decisions. You may want to share some of the great passages of our faith that tell us of God's open embrace to sinners: The story of the prodigal son comes to mind (Luke 15:11–32). Regardless of what the son has done, the father awaits the son's return with open arms. You may want to ask a trusted pastor to help you express your heart with true kindness.

A relationship with God brings us into his peace. Entering that relationship doesn't depend on anything we do. We can't earn God's love. God simply gives himself to us as a gift. We don't earn or buy his love by being good people. True, a Christian *expresses* her love to God by living according to the principles of the Bible. But *entering* a relationship is much more like standing at the altar during a wedding ceremony. Bride and groom each give their love to their lover, not expecting a payment of any sort. So just as the bride commits her life to her groom by saying "I do," so you can commit your life into God's care by responding to his invitation, by saying the "I do" of personal commitment to him. This is what the Bible calls *faith*.

Choosing to Die Well

We began with three responses to the case of an elderly man named Uncle Russ. His family members responded to his situation differently. His niece, Mary, wanted the physician to end his life in order to end their suffering. We think this amounts to *disposing of* someone. This includes all forms of euthanasia and PAS. We argue against *disposing of* humans made in God's image.

Jan, however, wanted the medical staff to do all they could for Uncle Russ. She refused to allow Uncle Russ to die. Out of respect for the sanctity of Uncle Russ's life, Jan wanted the doctor to treat him until the very end—keeping the physical body alive at all costs. We think this is really *holding on to* someone. We believe this is a naïve and unrealistic approach that strengthens the position of euthanasia proponents. It allows the euthanasia movement to play on Americans' fears of a long and drawn-out death to gather support for their alternative—legalized euthanasia.

The view we defend is an alternative that's often ignored when the two extreme positions are debated in the political arena. Steve, of course, represents this approach. He was willing to *let go of* Uncle Russ once it became clear that his life was ending and God was calling him to the next world. Steve rejected euthanasia, but he advocated allowing to die.

This "letting go" means refraining from attempts to cure end-stage, terminal disease, but it doesn't mean ceasing to care for the patient. It's a full-blooded commitment to *only* caring. We believe that under appropriate conditions, *letting go* is morally right for Christian physicians, pastors, and families.

The conditions are critical. We aren't justified in ceasing medical treatment just any time the doctor, the family, or even the patient wishes. No one has an absolute right to die in that sense. God is the Giver of life, and seeking death because life no longer seems worth living is a faithless act which throws the most precious gift possible—life itself—back in the face of the Giver. Thus *letting go* is appropriate when an end-stage terminal patient (or a representative) requests an end of treatments that won't cure the disease, allows the disease to run its course to death, and receives loving care for his physical, emotional, and spiritual needs until he dies. In cases that meet criteria like these, Christians who are terminally ill may rightly let go of life, say their farewells to loved ones, and prepare to meet the Creator.

Knowing fully the complexity of this bewildering

set of questions, we still believe Christians can choose to die well. We recognize our joyful duty to live for God throughout our lives and then accept, from a stance of hope, our desire to honor God in our dying. These decisions are difficult to make and even more troublesome to live out. Yet the Lord's promises that he will guide and sustain us are as true today as in the days of Jesus. Thus, with Paul we can say, not glibly, but with depth and understanding: "For to me, to live is Christ and to die is gain" (Philippians 1:21).

Notes

Chapter One

1. Katie Letcher Lyle, "A Gentle Way to Die," *Newsweek* (March 2, 1992): 14.
2. Stanley Hauerwas, *Naming the Silences* (Grand Rapids: Eerdmans, 1990), 60.
3. Even psychiatry, which touches the soulish part of humans, often diagnoses a disorder as physiological in cause and responds with medication that addresses the physical. Sometimes this is appropriate. But many psychiatrists and psychologists, for instance, never prescribe confession or prayer as a path to healing.
4. One of the most peculiar expressions in our political rhetoric is the statement that politicians should "fix the economy."
5. Daniel Callahan, *What Kind of Life?* (New York: Simon & Schuster, 1990), 242.
6. For a brief, helpful overview of holistic health from a Christian viewpoint, see Douglas R Groothuis, *Unmasking the New Age* (Downers Grove, Ill.: InterVarsity, 1986), 57–70.
7. For more on how laughter and biblical attitudes, for example, can contribute to healing, see William Backus, *The Healing Power of a Christian Mind* (Minneapolis: Bethany House Publishers, 1996).
8. Some thoughtful analysts describe the relationship between a Christian physician and patient as a *covenant*, e.g., Paul Ramsey, *The Patient*

as Person (New Haven: Yale University Press, 1970); William F. May, *The Physician's Covenant* (Philadelphia: Westminster Press, 1983).

9. Sometimes higher obligations negate this duty. For example, some say that in self-defense, a person may do harm to another while protecting innocent life. Saving innocent life is a higher duty than the command to do no harm. But in the absence of an overriding reason, humans shouldn't harm others.

10. David Thomasma, "The Basis of Medicine and Religion: Respect for Persons," *Linacre Quarterly* 47 (1984): 142–50.

11. Tom L. Beauchamp and James F. Childress, *Principles of Biomedical Ethics*, 2d ed. (New York: Oxford University Press, 1983), 59.

12. Landmark legal cases such as *Salgo* (1957), *Natason* (1960), and *Canterbury* (1972) helped propel the idea of informed consent into the foreground.

Chapter Two

1. To explore ethical theory from a Christian viewpoint, consult *Readings in Christian Ethics, Volume I: Theory and Method*, David K. Clark and Robert V. Rakestraw, eds. (Grand Rapids: Baker, 1994).

2. The best known popularizer of situationism is Joseph Fletcher, whose book *Situation Ethics* caused a sensation when it was first published (Philadelphia: Westminster Press, 1966). An evangelical theologian who defends *contextualism* is Donald Bloesch, although his view differs significantly from Fletcher's.

3. Fletcher, *Situation Ethics*, 164–65. In an appendix to *Situation Ethics*, Fletcher illustrates his view by citing the now famous case of Mrs. Bergmeier. A Soviet patrol picked up Mrs. Bergmeier as she scrounged for food for her family in the chaos after WWII. Later, in a prison camp in Ukraine, Mrs. Bergmeier learned that her family needed her in Berlin. The only way she could return to Germany, however, was to get pregnant, so she found a guard who willingly impregnated her. She then obtained release and found her way back to her family. Her family was overjoyed to see her alive. Later they welcomed little Dietrich as the one who made their reunion possible. Though Fletcher doesn't say so, he implies that this choice is morally commendable.

4. These ethical theories are called *teleological*, a word derived from the

Greek root *telos*, which means end, goal, or purpose.

5. This is known as *deontological* ethics.

6. William J. Bennett, *The Book of Virtues: A Treasury of Great Moral Stories* (New York: Simon & Schuster, 1993).

7. A leading exponent of virtue ethics in the world of theology is Duke University professor Stanley Hauerwas, author of *Vision and Virtue* (Notre Dame: Fides Publishers, 1974), 66.

8. Some call this three-part analysis the *act-intention complex*. Norman Geisler suggests this phrase, but he doesn't emphasize it in his writings on ethics.

9. These steps reflect the ideas of H. E. Tödt, "Towards a Theory of Making Ethical Judgments," *Journal of Religious Ethics* 6 (1978): 108–20.

10. Daniel C. Maguire calls this thinking through the "moral object." *Death by Choice* (Garden City: Image, 1984), 66–76.

Chapter Three

1. *Time* (August 2, 1993; August 23, 1993).

2. Jon D. Hull, "A Boy and His Gun," *Time* (August 23, 1993): 22.

3. Cited in Charles Colson, *The Body* (Waco, Tex.: Word, 1992), 175.

4. "The 'Animal Rights' War on Medicine," *Reader's Digest* (June 1990): 70–76.

5. David J. A. Clines shows from Hebrew word structure that the best way to render the phrase is "as God's image," not "in his image." He proves that the people of the ancient Near East thought of images as physical, three-dimensional objects. So an entire human person, body and soul, is an image. The image is also the dwelling place of the spirit whom it represents. Thus, to be the image of God is to represent God with one's entire body and soul. "The Image of God in Man," *Tyndale Bulletin* 19 (1968): 80.

6. They did, of course, become "like God" in that they knew good and evil (Genesis 3:22). There's irony here, however, for they thought they would become "like God" in a positive sense but instead became "like God" in experiencing evil for the first time.

7. On this definition of *person*, see Robert V. Rakestraw, "The Persistent Vegetative State and the Withdrawal of Nutrition and Hydration," *Journal of the Evangelical Theological Society* 35 (1992): 401.

8. Some philosophers discuss this issue using the concept of a *natural kind*. A *natural kind* is a class of objects that naturally possesses certain characteristics and abilities. The category to which something belongs indicates what attributes are appropriate for that thing. Being in the natural kind, *fish* means that a mackerel ought to have gills and live in water. Its possessing gills follows from its membership in the natural kind, *not the other way around*. Similarly, it's not the case that any creature having a certain level of intelligence is therefore human. A really smart chimp isn't human. Rather, a being is human because it's a member of the class of humankind. Because of this class membership, intelligence is appropriate for this being. But class membership—for example, being in the natural kind, *human*—is a given; it doesn't require a minimum IQ. Humanness isn't something to be earned. For an elaboration of this concept of natural kind, see David Wiggins, *Sameness and Substance* (Cambridge: Harvard University Press, 1980).

9. Walter C. Kaiser, Jr., *Toward Old Testament Ethics* (Grand Rapids: Academie, 1983), 91.

10. David K. Clark, "Philosophical Reflections on Self-Worth and Self-Love," *Journal of Psychology and Theology* 13 (1985): 3–11.

11. Paul Ramsey, *Patient as Person*, 154.

12. James Rachels, *The End of Life* (Oxford: Oxford University Press, 1986); for a competent refutation of Rachels' defense of euthanasia, see J. P. Moreland, "James Rachels and the Active Euthanasia Debate," *Journal of the Evangelical Theological Society* 31 (1988): 81–90.

13. Karl Barth, *Church Dogmatics*, Geoffrey Bromiley and T. F. Torrance, eds. (Edinburgh: T. & T. Clark, 1961), 3–4: 427.

14. See Matthew Conolly, "The Management of Cancer Pain," in *Suicide: A Christian Response*, Timothy J. Demy and Gary P. Stewart, eds. (Grand Rapids: Kregel, 1998), 75–99.

15. Paul Ramsey, *Ethics at the Edges of Life: Medical and Legal Intersections* (New Haven: Yale University Press, 1978), 146.

Chapter Four

1. Attributed to the sixteenth-century poet John Heywood.

2. Some Christians assume a three-part division of the human person into body, soul, and spirit. Only one verse, 1 Thessalonians 5:23, cites

exactly these three parts, and several texts mention four parts (e.g., Mark 12:30). These texts simply reference many facets of the human person; they're not tight lists of parts. So because the biblical evidence for a three-part view is weak, we reject it. The Bible usually assumes a twofold conception (e.g., Genesis 2:7; Ecclesiastes 12:7; Matthew 10:28, 26:41; Romans 8:10; 1 Corinthians 5:3; 2 Corinthians 7:1; James 2:26; 3 John 2). Both *soul* and *spirit* can refer to the nonphysical aspect of the human person, and we use the terms interchangeably. Millard Erickson calls the biblical perspective *conditional unity*. See *Christian Theology* (Grand Rapids: Baker, 1983–85), 536–39, for a brief description.

3. See Louis Berkhof, *Systematic Theology* (Grand Rapids: Eerdmans, 1953), 668, for an excellent discussion of this point.

4. Chaim Potok, *My Name Is Asher Lev* (New York: Ballantine, 1972), 150.

5. Erickson, *Christian Theology*, 1170–71.

6. James L. Bernat, Charles M. Culver, and Bernard Gert, "On the Definition and Criterion of Death," *Annals of Internal Medicine* 94 (1981): 389.

7. If we're not careful to keep *defining* and *diagnosing* death distinct, we can fall into a trap of using physical terms for both. For example, the medical community has accepted "having no reflexes" as a criterion for death. But now people describe "having no reflexes" as part of the *definition* of *death*. When this happens, we begin to see death as a purely physical thing, and the spiritual dimension is pushed to the background. We object to this language.

8. For clarity, note that this discussion is still about physical death. In saying that a definition of *death* must take account of the spiritual facet of the human person, we're not shifting the discussion to spiritual death. Physical death, we think, is best understood as an experience wherein the demise of physical systems coincides with the release of the soul into the next life. Spiritual death is a metaphor describing a person's alienation from God and is a different thing.

9. The various organs die at different times. The hair and nails continue to grow for 48 hours after the heart and lungs die. It's pointless to withhold the diagnosis of death until all organs are decaying. Once the brain is dead, no other organs can survive, and the organism is in the state of disintegration.

10. P. Mollaret and M. Goulon, "Le coma depasse," *Revue Neurologique* 101 (1959): 3.

11. "A Definition of Irreversible Coma," A Report of the Ad Hoc Committee of the Harvard Medical School, *Journal of the American Medical Association* 205 (August 1968): 337–40. Note two things: First, this is a definition of *irreversible coma*, not of *death*. Second, the presence of hypothermia (body core temperature less than 90° F.) or central nervous system depressant drugs such as barbiturates makes these criteria null.

12. Ramsey, *Patient As Person*, 101.

13. President's Commission, *Defining Death: Medical, Legal and Ethical Issues in the Determination of Death*, Morris B. Abram, Chair (Washington: U.S. Government Printing Office, 1981), 33. Notice that the title of this report wrongly speaks of *defining* death. Unfortunately, people commonly speak of the "Harvard definition." We prefer the phrase "Harvard criteria."

14. James L. Bernat, Charles M. Culver, and Bernard Gert, "Defining Death in Theory and Practice," *Hastings Center Report* 12 (1982): 5.

15. See Bryan Jennett and Fred Plum, "Persistent Vegetative State After Brain Damage: A Syndrome in Search of a Name," *Lancet* 1/7753 (1972): 734–37.

16. One patient lived in PVS for thirty-seven years. In some cases, women in PVS have delivered children. See D. Lamb, *Death, Brain Death, and Ethics* (Albany: SUNY Press, 1985).

17. This is the conclusion of Robert M. Veatch, *Death, Dying, and the Biological Revolution* (New Haven: Yale University Press, 1976), 48.

18. See "Pro-lifers Say Cruzan Death a Signal of Things to Come," *Christianity Today* (February 1, 1991): 56. Robert V. Rakestraw theologically defends the position that a PVS patient no longer possesses a spiritual self, is unable to image God, and may be allowed to die in "The Persistent Vegetative State," 389–405. Gilbert Meilaender defends the opposite perspective: "On Removing Food and Water: Against the Stream," *Hastings Center Report* 14 (December 1984): 11–13.

Chapter Five

1. Quoted in Charles Colson, "Aborting the Underclass," *Christianity Today* (June 22, 1992): 88.

2. Derek Humphry, *Final Exit* (Eugene, Ore.: The Hemlock Society, 1991).

3. George E. Lundberg, "Editorial," in *Journal of the American Medical Association* 259 (1988): 2143.

4. *Final Exit*, 62.

5. The United States Supreme Court (reversing judgments from the Second and Ninth Circuits) ruled that in spite of the equal protection and the due process clauses of the Fourteenth Amendment, states are permitted to make it a crime to aid a suicide, including when such assistance takes the form of a physician prescribing lethal medication to a competent, terminally ill adult who voluntarily requests the physician's help.

6. James Rachels, "Euthanasia," *Matters of Life and Death: New Introductory Essays in Moral Philosophy*, Tom Regan, ed. (Philadelphia: Temple University Press, 1980), 29.

7. See Rachels, *End of Life*.

8. There are various ways to make this kind of distinction. We see the end or goal that is chosen or intended as key. See Robert F. Weir, ed., *Ethical Issues in Death and Dying*, 2nd ed. (New York: Columbia University Press, 1986), 243–44.

9. If treatment were refused a long time before an underlying disease proved terminal, or if the certainty of death were inconclusive, then the decision to forgo further treatment would be tantamount to suicide.

10. Richard A. McCormick describes what he calls the "absolutization of autonomy." See "Physician-Assisted Suicide: Flight From Compassion," *Christian Century* (December 4, 1991): 1132–34.

11. See Millard J. Erickson and Ines E. Bowers, "Euthanasia and Christian Ethics," *Journal of the Evangelical Theological Society* 19 (1976): 15–24.

12. See Edmund D. Pellegrino, "Doctors Must Not Kill," *Journal of Clinical Ethics* 3 (1992): 95–102.

13. Idem, "Euthanasia and Assisted Suicide," in *Dignity and Dying*, John F. Kilner, ed., Arlene B. Miller, and Edmund D. Pellegrino (Grand Rapids: Eerdmans, 1996), 109–110.

14. Robert D. Orr, "Why Doctors Should Not Kill," *CMDS Journal* (Spring 1993), 14.

15. Paul J. van der Maas, et al., "Euthanasia, Physician-Assisted Suicide,

and Other Medical Practices Involving the End of Life in the Netherlands, 1990–1995," *New England Journal of Medicine* 335 (1996): 1699–1705.

16. Daniel Callahan, *What Kind of Life: The Limits of Medical Progress* (Washington, D.C.: Georgetown University Press, 1990), 242.

17. See Daniel Callahan and Margot White, "The Legalization of Physician-Assisted Suicide: Creating a Regulatory Potemkin Village," *University of Richmond Law Review* 30 (1996): 1–83, for a discussion of safeguards and their weaknesses. The safeguards mean that PAS is allowed only in cases where: incurable disease brings extensive suffering, reasonable attempts to alleviate pain fail, the assistance is requested by a patient whose judgment isn't impaired, adequate attempts are made to treat depression, and a second opinion confirms the terminal diagnosis. Safeguards of this sort are included in the Oregon law permitting PAS.

18. Paul J. van der Maas, Johannes J. M. van Delden, Lois Pijnenborg, Caspar W. N. Looman, "Euthanasia and Other Medical Decisions Concerning the End of Life," *Lancet* 338 (1991): 669–74.

19. Pellegrino, "Doctors Must Not Kill," 95–102.

Chapter Six

1. Jack Kevorkian, quoted by Joni Eareckson Tada, "Life and Death Decisions," *World* (May 21, 1994): 12.

2. There is no moral or legal difficulty with ceasing at time B a treatment that was started at time A—if the treatment isn't contributing to the patient's welfare at time B and *would not have been started* at time B. There's no command from God to continue futile treatments.

3. For the skilled clinician, this isn't as difficult a task as many insist. When a physician has cared for a patient through the course of an illness, the end stages can be quite well defined. Should the approaching end not be obvious, of course, the appropriate course is to err on the side of life.

4. Paul Ramsey, *Patient as Person*, 113–64.

5. Ibid., 151.

6. Ibid., 134.

7. Cicely Saunders and Mary Bains, *Living With Dying: The Management of Terminal Disease*, 2nd ed. (Oxford: Oxford University Press, 1989).

8. Ibid., 21–42.

9. Ibid., 43–56.

10. Cicely Saunders, "Caring to the End," *Nursing Mirror* (September 4, 1980): 52–53.

11. See "Consent as a Canon of Loyalty" in Ramsey, *Patient As Person*, 1–58.

12. *Maine Revised Statutes Annotated*, vol. 10, title 18a, sections 5–802.

13. The decision-maker may work in one of two ways: *substituted judgment* and *best interests*. In a *substituted judgment*, the proxy considers what *that patient* would have wanted. In a *best interests* judgment, the substitute considers what *a reasonable person* would choose. What *a particular person would want* and what *a reasonable person would choose* may not be the same. Jehovah's Witnesses reject blood transfusions, but most Americans don't. So a proxy operating under the substituted judgment criterion shouldn't choose a transfusion for a Witness; one using the best interests standard should.

Chapter Seven

1. God can and does heal. He heals out of compassion and mercy, to bring glory to himself as revealed in Jesus, and in response to our faith and his own promise. But he doesn't always heal, and we can't know all the specific reasons why. See Jack Deere, *Surprised by the Power of the Spirit* (Grand Rapids: Zondervan, 1993), chapters 9 and 11, for a biblical discussion of why God heals and why he sometimes doesn't.

2. David Hume, *Dialogues Concerning Natural Religion* (Indianapolis: Hackett, 1980), 63.

3. Peter Kreeft, *Making Sense Out of Suffering* (Ann Arbor: Servant Books, 1986), 27–44.

4. A full discussion of the various attempts to answer the intellectual problem of evil is beyond the purpose of this brief chapter. For a good introduction to various attempts to answer the problem of evil, see chapter 2 in Kreeft's *Making Sense Out of Suffering*, "Ten Easy Answers." You can find a sophisticated discussion of these issues in Michael L. Peterson, ed., *The Problem of Evil: Selected Readings* (Notre Dame: University of Notre Dame Press, 1992).

5. Kreeft, *Making Sense Out of Suffering*, 132.

6. Jesus clearly taught that a particular individual's suffering isn't necessarily due to that person's past sins (John 9:3).
7. R. C. Sproul, *The Invisible Hand* (Dallas: Word, 1996), 1.

Chapter Eight

1. Ruth Kopp, *When Someone You Love Is Dying* (Grand Rapids: Zondervan, 1980), 18–55.
2. John Dunlop, "A Physician's Advice to Spiritual Counselors of the Dying," *Trinity Journal* 14 (1993): 203.
3. Philip Yancey, *Disappointment With God: Three Questions No One Asks Aloud* (Grand Rapids: Zondervan, 1988), 192.
4. James Dobson, *When God Doesn't Make Sense* (Wheaton: Tyndale, 1993), 25–42.
5. Frederick Buechner, *Wishful Thinking* (New York: Harper & Row, 1973), 46–47.
6. The original source of this analogy is a "Dear Abby" column.
7. This is a significant theme in several writings of C. S. Lewis. For example, see *The Great Divorce* (New York: Macmillan, 1946), 67–68.
8. Max Lucado, *Tell Me the Secrets: Treasures for Eternity* (Wheaton: Crossway, 1993), 60–61.
9. Hauerwas, *Naming the Silences*, 98–99.
10. Paul's words here quote Isaiah 25:8 and Hosea 13:14.
11. Thomas N. Finger, *Christian Theology: An Eschatological Approach*, vol. 1 (Nashville: Thomas Nelson, 1985), 142.

Chapter Nine

1. Alister E. McGrath, *The Mystery of the Cross* (Grand Rapids: Zondervan, 1988), 161.